GAMES OF
MANY NATIONS

GAMES OF
MANY NATIONS

E. O. Harbin

ABINGDON PRESS

Nashville
New York

GAMES OF MANY NATIONS

ISBN 0-687-13990-2

Library of Congress Catalog Card Number: 54-8238

SET UP, PRINTED, AND BOUND BY THE
PARTHENON PRESS, AT NASHVILLE,
TENNESSEE, UNITED STATES OF AMERICA

DEDICATED TO the "goodly fellowship" of missionaries and other workers the world around who give their lives to the cause of world brotherhood

INTRODUCTION

THIS IS A COLLECTION of games that are played the world around. They may be played by all age groups—children, youth, and adults. Boy Scouts, Girl Scouts, and similar organizations; church groups; and other organizations interested in developing the spirit of world brotherhood will find them helpful. They might be used successfully in various programs such as "A World Playday," "A Trip Around the World," and so on. Folk dances have not been included because there are many source books containing them.

As you play these games, try to come to a friendly appreciation of the people from whom they come. In these days of world tension it is well to remind ourselves of the kinship of men everywhere. This kinship is apparent as you note the similarities in games played in different nations.

"Blindman's Buff" is a universal favorite. In Russia and Greece it is played exactly as it is in the United States. In China there is a slight variation, the players stooping to avoid being caught. In Africa there is another variation, two players being blindfolded, with the runner indicating his position by striking two sticks together.

"Drop the Handkerchief" is played in Italy, Greece, Japan, and Russia. In Japan it is called "Hankachiotoshi."

"Hide and Seek" under various names is played in most European countries. In France it is called "Cache Cache." "How Do You Like Your Neighbor?" is played in the Balkans and in Turkey, and there is mention of its being played in Constantinople as early as 1649. "Jintori" in Japan is the same as "Prisoner's Base" in the United States. "Going to Jerusalem," or "Musical Chairs," is played in Germany under the name of "Mauer Blumchen" (wallflower). "Sonca" (emphasis on the last syllable) means "toss." It is a Philippine Island version of "Jacks." Six hard fruits, stones, or marbles are used for the jacks. In India this game is called "Guttak" (emphasis on the last syllable), and five hard, round beans are used. "Pum-Pum-Pulloi," as played in the Philippines, is the same as our "Pom-Pom-Pullaway." "Last Couple Out," a game we play in the United States, is played in Russia under the name of "Gorelki," in Scotland as "Widower," and in Africa, where it is called "Kholo Eveawo." "Quatre Coins," literally "four corners," is the French name for "Pussy Wants a Corner." The French also play "Saute-Mouton" ("Leapfrog"), "Colin-Maillard" ("Blindman's Buff"), and "Pigeon Voli" ("Birds Fly").

It is interesting to note the origins of many games. "Prisoner's Base" and "Stealing Sticks" date back to the first Olympics. "Croquet" originated in France, where it was known as "Pall-Mall"; and from there it went to England, where it gave its name to the famous street in London called "Pall Mall." "Hide and Seek" grew out of an early custom in which people went out in the spring to find birds, flowers, or insects to bring back as evidence of the coming of the season. In some European countries the hiders imitate birds to tip off the hunters, thus reflecting the background of the game. I had always thought "Chinese

Checkers" was an adaptation of the old Swedish game "Helma."
However, Dr. Liu I Hsin insists that it has an authentic Chinese
background. He says he played it as a child and that his grandfather and his grandfather's grandfather played it before him.
He says that in China the game is played with fifteen marbles in
each corner, while "Helma" is played with ten marbles and there
are only two players in the game at a time.

"Badminton" is the ancient game of "Poona" from India.
More than two thousand years ago it was played in the Orient.
An English army officer introduced it to his friends on his estate
in England. The estate happened to bear the title "Badminton,"
so from then on that's what the game was called. Tennis was born
in France. Bowling was introduced into the United States by the
Dutch settlers. Plato credits football to the Egyptians, and Hol-
land and Scotland both claim credit for golf. Basketball, volleyball, and modern baseball originated in the United States, although baseball is a close relative of the old English game of
"Rounders."

I am deeply grateful for the help in the preparation of this
material that I received from many persons around the world.
Miss Alberta Tarr, of Hiroshima, Japan, is responsible for most
of the games from Japan. The Rev. Asa W. Mellinger, of Chico-
pee, Massachusetts, is a minister who follows anthropology as
a hobby and in doing so has discovered a number of games
from many countries, of which he has contributed to this book
the following: "African Simon Says," "African Game Trap,"
"Jarabadach," "Spear the Whale," "Leopards and Cattle," and
a variation of "Scissors Chess." Miss Helen Johnson, of New
York City, has contributed much also and has been most helpful
in suggesting missionaries to contact for contributions. For the
games they contributed to the collection my appreciation is
here expressed to others, as follows: William M. Holt, of

Cochabamba, Bolivia, for "Juego del Panuelo," "Paloma y Gavilan," and "La Palma"; Lois Davidson, of Iquique, Chile, for "The King's Messenger," "Va El Tren," "La Canasta," and "Cambio de Instrumentos"; J. W. Dyson for "Fist Slinging" and "Pick-Up Race"; H. L. Li, of Taiwan, China, for "Throwing the Square," "Clasping for Seven," "Catching Seven Pieces," and "Spreading the Fist"; Gene Hibbard, of Windham, Ohio, for "Da Err," "Chinese Hopscotch," and "Chinese Stick Rhythms"; Christine Evans, of Holguin, Cuba, for "The Fans," "The Dogs and the Chickens," "Doña Ana," "Cuba and Spain," "Asi Jugaba Porque Jugue," and "Matandile"; Christine Evans and Ione Clay, of Cuba, for "La Marisola"; Peter Olsen, of Minneapolis, Minn., for "Stykes"; Marcelle Mancuit for "La-Marelle"; Patricia McHugh, of Honolulu, Hawaii, for "Pahee," "Noa," "Puhenehene," and "Loulou"; Arthur W. Howard, of Lucknow, India, for "Kho-Kho," "Sia Mar Danda," and "Gooli Danda"; Kuribashi, a Japanese student, for a variation of "Scissors Chess" and "Five Eyes"; Fujino Atsuko and Tomito Mayumi, of Hiroshima, Japan, for "Big Lantern, Little Lantern" and "Rakansan"; S. Truda, of Hiroshima, for "Foreigner"; Hiroko Yagi and Shimako Hashimoto, of Hiroshima, for "Karutatori"; Seiko Ashiwa, of Hiroshima, for "Poem Card Playing"; Yuriko Sakai and Miyoka Morimoto, of Hiroshima, for "Sugoroku"; Yoko Animoto, of Hiroshima, for "Kagome-Kagome"; Takako Twane and Chizue Suga, of Hiroshima, for "Takaratori"; Fuijiko Yamada, of Hiroshima, for "Otedama"; Junko Masumoto, of Hiroshima, for "Hanakago"; Leonor Arce for "Little Clown" and "The Little Ball"; Carol Moe, of Bayombong, P. I., for "San Pedro and San Pablo"; Violeta Cavallero, of Montevideo, Uruguay, for "The Color Market," "The Blind Hen," and "The Wolf."

E. O. HARBIN

CONTENTS

Africa 15

Alaska 20

American Indian 22

Bolivia 27

Brazil 30

Burma 33

Ceylon 34

Chile 36

China 40

Cuba 55

Denmark 71

England 75

France 79

Germany 81

Greece 83

Hawaii 85

India 88

Italy 99

Japan 104

Korea 119

Malaya 124

Mexico 127

Persia 131

Peru 132

Philippines 135

Russia 139

Scotland 141

Uruguay 145

Forfeits 148

Game Index 153

Classified Index 157

GAMES OF
MANY NATIONS

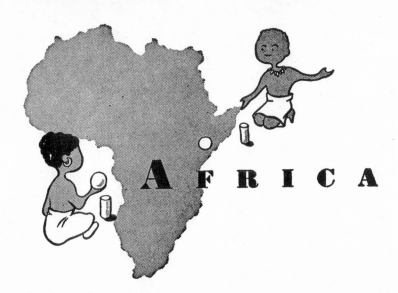

A F R I C A

MULAMBILWA

Number of players: Two teams of five to nine each.

Formation and equipment: Teams kneel facing each other about fifteen or twenty feet apart. In front of each player is a tenpin or pop bottle. Each player has a ball.

Action: At the signal to start, each player throws or rolls his ball at the pin of some opponent. When all pins are down for one team, the members of that team must get up and run to their goal, a line about twenty or thirty feet away. If caught, they must pay forfeits or receive roughing from their captors. ·

AFRICAN BLINDMAN'S BUFF

Number of players: Five or more.

Formation: Circle, with two blindfolded players inside.

Action: One of the blindfolded players has two sticks which he must hit together often to indicate where he is. Instruct him to keep his sticks low so the other blindfolded player, who is "It," will not be stuck in the face if he runs into them. Usually "It" has a piece of cloth which he waves in the effort to locate the stick-man. When "It" tags the stickman, that person becomes "It" and a new stickman is chosen.

NSIKWI

Number of players: Two or more.

Formation: Two players or two teams sit on the ground facing each other, about ten feet apart. In front of each player is a piece of corncob about two or three inches high. An empty bottle or any other light thing may be substituted for the corncob.

Action: Each player has a top (or ball). When all players are ready, each one sends his top or ball on the ground across the intervening space with great force, trying to knock down the corncob of his opponent. Each hit registers a point.

HEN AND WILDCAT

Number of players: Five or more.

Formation and action: One player is chosen as the hen and another as the wildcat. The rest of the players are the chickens. The hen leads the chickens around and warns them of any approaching danger. The wildcat hides himself. At unexpected times and places he springs out and tries to catch any foolish chicken who fails to drop to the ground at the mother hen's warning. This may continue until all chickens are caught, or a new hen and a new wildcat may be chosen whenever a chicken is caught.

CATTLE STOCKADE

This game is very similar to our "Bull in the Ring."

Number of players: Twelve or more.

Formation and action: Players form a circle, hands clasped, around one or more players. These inside players represent the cattle. They hold up their hands and rush against the "stockade," trying to break through. If they succeed, the players responsible for the break-through become the cattle.

LION AND DEER TAG

Number of players: Five or more.

Formation and action: This is played just like tag except that "It" is the lion and the rest of the players are deer.

AFRICAN HANDBALL

Number of players: Six or more.

Action: Players are divided into two equal teams. The game is started by a member of one team tossing a ball to one of his own side. The object of the game is for a team to keep possession of the ball as long as possible. The other team tries to intercept it and gain possession of it.

Every time the ball is caught, the members of that team, except the player catching the ball, clap their hands and stamp their feet.

AFRICAN SIMON SAYS

Number of players: Four or more.

Formation: A leader faces the other players, who stand in a straight line in front of him.

Action: This game may be played in two ways:

1. The leader faces one player in the line. Each of them raises his arms above his head and claps his hands together. Suddenly the leader thrusts one of his arms out in front of him as if striking a blow. The other player must respond immediately by bringing forward his corresponding arm—right

17

must match right; left must match left. If he brings forward the wrong arm, the leader wins. On an agreed number of wins the leader becomes a chief and retires from the game.

2. The leader stands before the entire group. All players follow him in what he does. A player who makes a mistake takes the leader's place, and the leader joins the group. If several players make mistakes, the leader points out the one to take his place.

AFRICAN GAME TRAP

This is similar to the game of "Arches," in which the players march to music, the bridge falling when the music stops.
Number of players: Fifteen to one hundred.
Formation: Players form a single circle. Two players take hold of hands and form a bridge or "trap" under which the other players must march.
Action: The marchers sing or chant as they clap their hands rhythmically:

> Lions and leopards, lions and leopards,
>> Hunting at night;
> Lions and leopards, lions and leopards,
>> Catch the game!

The "trap" falls upon the word "game."

Players caught form additional "traps." The game continues until all players have been caught. Players must move in rhythm, not pausing or dashing through to keep from getting caught.

JARABADACH

This game is somewhat similar to "Ticktacktoe."
Number of players: Two.

Equipment: One player has three white stones or markers, and the other has three black ones. The game is played on a diagram marked on the ground or on paper. This diagram is in the form of a large square divided into four small squares by two lines. The plays are made on the nine points of this large square.

1	2	3
4	5	6
7	8	9

Action: Players take turns in placing their markers, one at a time, on any of the nine points of the square. The purpose is to get three in a row before the opponent can. After the six pieces are placed, players take turns in moving along the lines, a space at a time, until one of the players wins.

SPEAR THE WHALE,
OR ESKIMO ESCAPADES

Number of players: Two.

Equipment: A diamond-shaped piece of plywood four inches wide and six inches long. In the center of this piece is a hole one inch in diameter. In the Arctic this piece is cut from whalebone and the block at the end from walrus tusk. This block is rectangular and may be made of a piece of pine. If of pine, then it should be two inches by three inches by four inches, to be the proper weight. Thus the block would vary in size, depending on the kind of material used. Strings are attached to the ends of the diamond as indicated in the diagram. One string connects the block with the diamond. The other string is suspended from a doorway, bar, or tree limb, so that the hole in the diamond-shaped piece is waist high.

Two wands, each twenty inches long, must be made. The ends should be blunt and rounded, and small enough to slip easily into the hole in the diamond. Sandpaper the wands so they will be smooth to handle.

Draw two parallel lines five feet apart, with the diamond-shaped piece suspended midway between the lines. For children the parallel lines may be closer together. However, see that they are far enough apart so that there will be no danger of players striking each other with their wands.

Action: Each player attempts to thrust his wand through the hole, and at the same time he tries to keep his opponent from doing likewise. Sounds easy, does it? Just try it! Play for the best two out of three or the best three out of five points.

BALL RACE

Equipment: A ball for each player. The Indians use a five-
or six-inch ball of wood or stone covered with mesquite gum.
A volleyball or play ball may be used.

Action: Players engage in a foot race in which they kick the
ball ahead of them. A player has not finished the course until
both he and the ball are over the goal line. Touching the ball
with the hands disqualifies a player.

Variation: Use a football. This will make it harder to keep
the ball in the course.

WHERE IS THE STICK?

Number of players: Six or more.

Equipment: Two small sticks about the size and shape of a
piece of chalk. One of these sticks is marked by a white or black
stripe, a notch, or some other mark so as to distinguish it from
the other.

Formation: Players are divided into two equal sides. They

sit facing one another about two feet apart. The leader on one side holds the two sticks. He changes them from one hand to the other, putting his hands back of him once in a while and trying to keep the sticks from being seen.

Action: When the leader indicates he is ready, the players on the opposing team try to guess which hand holds the marked stick. One player at a time guesses. If he guesses correctly, he becomes the leader and the other side guesses. If he guesses incorrectly, the game continues with the same leader manipulating the sticks. When three wrong guesses have been made, the sticks change sides.

PIMA STICKS

Number of players: Two or more.

Equipment: A set of four sticks six to nine inches long and one to two inches wide and two slender marking sticks about a foot long. The four Pima sticks are flat on one side and rounded on the other like yoot sticks (see page 122). On the flat side they are marked by carved lines filled with black paint (see diagram). The other side is rounded and painted red. A space ten feet square is enclosed by holes as in diagram.

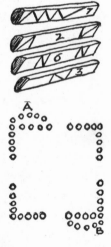

Action: A player (or team) places his marking stick in the corner hole at *A*. The opponent (or opposing team) puts his marking stick in the corner hole at *B*. The object of the game is to move the marking stick around the square, hole by hole. The first one around wins. The moving is determined by tossing the four Pima sticks up in the air, all at one time. They indicate the score as follows: Four round sides up count 10; four flat sides up count 5; only one flat side up counts whatever its marking indicates—7, 6, 3, or 2 (see diagram). The player moves his marking stick accordingly. *A* moves to the right around the arch, then returns to the first hole at the top of the square and moves all around the square. *B* moves to the left around the arch and then to the right around the square. Whenever the count brings the marking stick to a hole occupied by the stick of an opponent, that opponent is sent back to the starting point. Passing an opponent does not send him "home."

ARROW GAME

Number of players: Six or more.

Formation: Two teams of equal numbers line up about forty feet from a target. This target is an arrow standing upright against a hillside.

Action: Players from the two teams alternate in shooting with bow and arrow at the arrow on the hill. The one who hits the target or who comes closest to it scores a point for his team.

Variations: Substitute a slingshot for the bow and arrow, or use a ball, with a stick, piece of cardboard, or other marker for the target.

BUCKSKIN BALL

Number of players: Ten or more.

Equipment: The ball may be a large buckskin ball, a volley-ball, or a softball. Each player has a branch four or five feet long, containing a knot or bend at one end.

Formation: Two teams of equal numbers arrange themselves over the playing field as players do for the game of hockey. The two captains stand at center on the dividing line between the two goals. These goals are about one hundred feet on each side of the dividing line. They are indicated by buffalo robes, one at each end, or by some other appropriate marker.

Action: The ball is thrown between the captains on the dividing line. Each team tries to get it over the opponent's buffalo robe by the use of the sticks.

PAPAGO

Number of players: Two to twenty.

Equipment: Four cups or cones and a small object such as a bean or a marble.

Action: If there are more than two players, they divide into two teams. One of the players takes the four cones, conceals the bean or marble in one of them, and then fills them all with sand. He gives the filled cups to his opponent or to the opposing team. The opponent hands them back one at a time. If the first one handed back contains the hidden bean, the player who filled the cups scores ten points. If the bean is in the second cup, he scores six points. The third one counts four points, and the fourth counts nothing. The opponent or other team then hides the bean, and the game continues. Fifty points is out.

TOKINAWAS, OR RING AND ARROW

Number of players: Four.

Equipment: A ring seven inches in diameter made of dry corn husks, wrapped half with white and half with red cord. Four darts made of corncobs, each with two feathers in one end and a wooden point ten inches long in the other.

Action: Two players face each other, six to ten feet apart. They roll the ring back and forth. The other two players on opposite sides throw their darts, one at a time, at the moving ring. The player who hits the ring or shoots through it oftenest in ten trials wins.

BATTLEDORE AND SHUTTLECOCK

This is somewhat similar to "Badminton."

Number of players: Five or more.

Equipment: A battledore for each player. This is a circular piece of wood about nine inches in diameter, with a wooden handle. A ping-pong paddle will do. The shuttlecock could be a badminton bird or a large cork with three feathers stuck in it.

Formation: Circle, with players about six to ten feet apart.

Action: A player starts by batting the shuttlecock to his neighbor to the right. That player must keep it going by batting it to the next player to his right. When a player fails to hit a fair serve, he is out. The game continues until only one man is left. If a player knocks the shuttlecock over the head of another player, he drops out and not the player who was unable to reach it.

KICK THE STICK RELAY

Number of players: Six or more.

Formation and action: Two teams line up in relay formation at a starting line. In front of each team is a crooked stick about twelve inches long. The first player kicks the stick to the goal and back. The stick must be kicked along the ground, not in the air. The first player leaves the stick in front of the next player on his team. That player repeats the performance. The first team to have all its runners complete the course wins.

JUEGO DEL PANUELO
(Handkerchief Game)

Number of players: Sixteen to thirty-two.

Formation: Cross.

Action: The players are seated in two lines forming a cross (see diagram). One person is elected to be "It." This person circles the group and drops the handkerchief behind the person seated at the end of one of the lines. When the handkerchief is dropped, everyone in that particular line (eight in the above diagram) must circle the group and return to his seat. In the meantime "It" takes one of the vacated seats. Of course, when players return to their seats, the last person arriving is without a seat, and he becomes "It." The game is continued as long as desired.

PALOMA Y GAVILAN

(The Eagle and the Pigeon)

This game is similar to our "Cat and Rat."

Number of players: Eight or more.

Action: One person is chosen to be the eagle. Another is chosen to be the pigeon. All the others form a circle and join hands. The eagle chases the pigeon about the circle. Those who make up the circle are on the side of the pigeon and let him pass under their clasped hands. They try not to let the eagle come through. The game lasts until the eagle catches the pigeon or gives up trying.

LA PALMA

Number of players: Two or more.

Equipment: This game is very popular with the Indians of Bolivia who live either on the Altiplano or down in the tropical lowlands. The only equipment needed (or used by them) is a tail bone of a donkey or a llama (a stick may be used) and several rocks. The bone is stuck in the ground for a target. A line is made in the ground about three yards from the bone. Other lines are made, each about three yards farther from the bone than the preceding line. There are about six lines in all, with the last being eighteen yards from the bone.

Action: The players (usually boys) take turns, standing first at line number one, with their slings and try to hit the bone with a rock. In case they do not have slings, they merely throw rocks. If the person is successful in hitting the bone at line number one, he moves on to line number two. The first person to hit the bone from all six lines wins the game. When the players are very good with their slings, they sometimes double the distance between lines.

CAT AND RAT

This is similar to our "Cat and Rat."

Number of players: Ten or more.

Formation: The other players form a circle, hands clasped. Two players represent the cat and rat. The cat stands outside the circle and the rat inside.

Action: The Brazilian game, however, adds a very interesting feature. The cat knocks on the back of one of the players in the circle. That player asks, "What do you want?"

"I want to see the rat," replies the cat.

"You cannot see him now," says the circle player.

"When can I see him?" asks the cat.

"At ten o'clock," comes the reply. (The player can call out any time he desires.)

Immediately the circle begins moving around in rhythm as they count off the hours. All the players may call off the hours. Thus they call, "One o'clock, ticktock! Two o'clock, ticktock!

Three o'clock, ticktock!" and so on, until they reach the announced time, which in this case is ten o'clock. At this point the circle stops moving. The cat steps up again to the player whose back he tapped. He knocks again. This time the dialogue is as follows: "What do you want?"

"I want to see the rat."

"What time is it?"

"Ten o'clock!" answers the cat.

"All right; come in!"

The cat ducks in, and the rat tries to elude him by getting outside. From there on it is played just as the American game.

In moving around, while counting off the hours, players should make an effort to get good rhythm. By taking two steps between each call and two steps while making the call, they can do this.

HIT THE PENNY

(Also many other South American countries)

Number of players: Two or more.

Equipment: A bamboo stick, twelve to eighteen inches long, is set up in the ground. A piece of broomstick may be substituted, if bamboo is not available. On top of the bamboo is placed a penny or other coin, or a metal washer. The stick is in the center of a circle about three feet in diameter. This circle is marked on the ground. If the game is played indoors, the coin may be placed on a stool and the circle may be indicated by a string.

Action: Players stand at a distance of four to six feet and take turns trying to knock the coin off the bamboo by throwing a penny at it. If they knock it off and outside the three-foot circle, they score one point. If it drops inside the circle or if they miss it, they score nothing.

31

MORRAL, OR GRAB BAG

(Also many other South American countries)

Number of players: Any number.

Equipment: A large sack or container filled with enough gifts for everyone in the group. These gifts may be comical or otherwise.

Action: Players, in turn, reach into the grab bag and take out a present. Sometimes mottoes, fortunes, or verses are used instead of presents. In this case they are read by those who draw them, for the amusement of the crowd.

Variation: If desired, suggestions for stunts to be performed may be placed on slips of paper, perhaps in small envelopes. (See section on forfeits, page 148, for ideas for stunts.) The persons drawing them must perform, as directed, for the entertainment of the group.

LOO K'BAH ZEE

Number of players: Six or more.

Formation: Players form a straight line, holding their hands open behind them. One player is back of the line.

Action: The player back of the line holds a stone or other small object (a marble perhaps) in his hand. He walks up and down pretending to put the object in a player's hands. Finally he does drop it into a player's hands. That player darts out of the line, trying to avoid being tagged by those on either side of him. The taggers may not move out of their places, but must catch him as he leaves his place. If the runner is not caught, he goes back to his own place and the game continues. If he is caught, he exchanges places with the player behind the line.

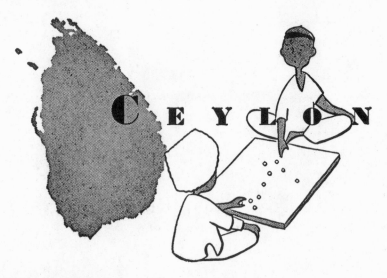

DIVIYAN KELIYA, OR
LEOPARDS AND CATTLE

This is somewhat similar to "Fox and Geese."

Number of players: Two.

Equipment: A board ten to twelve inches square marked as indicated in the diagram. Care should be taken to see that all lines are properly placed. If desired, holes may be drilled at the forty-nine points of intersection, and marbles may be used for the cattle and leopards. Otherwise use twenty-four counters (checkers) for the cattle and two of contrasting color for the leopards.

Action: One player takes the twenty-four cattle. His opponent uses the two leopards. The object of the game is for the cattle to pen the leopards so they cannot be moved or for the leopards to "eat up" (jump) the cattle.

To start the game, a leopard is placed at the center intersection. One of the cattle is then placed anywhere on the board, followed by the second leopard, which also may be placed on any vacant spot on the board.

Play alternates, the cattle being placed one at a time. Between each placement the leopard may either jump, if a jump is possible, or else move along one of the marked lines from the spot occupied to an adjacent empty spot.

Cattle cannot be moved until they have all been placed. They may then move one space at a time along the lines to an adjacent empty space.

A leopard may "eat up" one of the cattle by jumping over it from an adjacent space to an empty space beyond, along one of the lines. Double or triple jumps, as in checkers, are permitted. A jump cannot be refused. Cattle cannot jump. Leopards may jump backward, forward, or sideways along the lines.

Cattle win if both leopards are completely cornered. Leopards win if they "eat up" enough cattle (usually ten) so that they cannot be cornered.[1]

---

[1] This is an ancient game, handed down through the centuries from one generation to the next. The fact that it is still played is some indication of its worth.

CHILE

LA BARRA

Number of players: Eight or more.

Formation: Two teams of players line up in one straight line. In front of them, about twenty feet away, stands "It," one player of one of the teams.

Action: The opposing team to "It's" team shouts the question "Barra?" When someone from the other team answers, "Dicha la Barra!" a player runs out from the team that shouted the question and tries to tag "It." At the same time a player runs out from the opposing team and tries to tag the runner before he touches "It." If the runner succeeds in touching "It" before being tagged himself, "It" becomes a prisoner. If the runner is tagged himself, however, before he reaches "It," he becomes prisoner.

The other team then sends one of its men out to stand twenty feet away, and the game continues. The game ends when one team has only one player left.

THE KING'S MESSENGER

Number of players: Eight to twelve.

Formation: Circle or line.

Action: Each player is given the name of a color—Red, Blue, Yellow, and so forth—and one player is the king's messenger. The king's messenger enters and says that the king has been robbed and one of the players is the guilty person. There is a pattern to the dialogue, and a forfeit has to be paid for each mistake made. A mistake is made when any player answers out of turn or when a player hesitates too long before answering the king's messenger. The dialogue goes thus:

> *K. M.:* I have come to say that the king has lost a gold ring and that Red has it.
>
> *Red:* I, my Lord?
>
> *K. M.:* Yes, my Lord.
>
> *Red:* No, my Lord.
>
> *K. M.:* Then who has it?
>
> *Red:* Yellow has it.

The dialogue is repeated until all the players have been asked for the gold ring, after which players retrieve the objects they forfeited by doing some kind of stunt (see section on forfeits, page 148).

VA EL TREN

Number of players: Eight to twenty.

Formation: The players are seated in a circle on the ground or floor.

Action: A small stone is passed from hand to hand as they sing the song *Va El Tren*. When they get to the word *chiquichiquicha* (pronounced "chicky-chicky-chaw"), the player who has the stone in his hand retains it until the word is finished. Keeping time to the music and to the three parts of the word (as indicated in the pronunciation above), he touches the ground three times with the stone, first directly in front of himself, then a little way forward, and then back to the original spot. If any player forgets to touch the stone to the ground three times, in time to the music and the word, he has to drop out of the game. The game continues until all are out.[2]

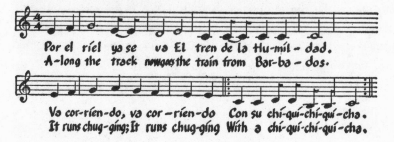

Por el riel ya se va El tren de la Hu-mil-dad.
A-long the track now goes the train from Bar-ba-dos.

Va cor-rien-do, va cor-rien-do Con su chi-qui-chi-qui-cha.
It runs chug-ging; It runs chug-ging With a chi-qui-chi-qui-cha.

LA CANASTA

Number of players: Ten or more.

Formation: Circle.

Action: This game is like our game "Fruit Basket" except that "It" begins by saying, "I have just been to the fruit market, and I bought limes, oranges," and so on. In Chile the "market" is really a market, a whole square block of stalls, so the connotation of the word "market" is considerably different there. When "It" calls out the fruits he has bought, the players bearing these names must immediately change places, or chairs if they are used. "It" tries to get one of the places, and if he succeeds, the player left without a place automatically becomes "It."

---

[2] A game similar to this may be found in my *Fun Encyclopedia*, pp. 491-92. It is entitled "You Must Pass This Spoon." A game like it is played in the Netherlands, except that there each player takes off his shoe and passes it to his neighbor to the right. On the words "do just what I do" the player taps the floor with the shoe to the right, to the left, and back to the right, and then on to the next player in the circle.

CAMBIO DE INSTRUMENTOS

Number of players: Eight or more.

Formation: Circle.

Action: "It" leaves the room. Each player is given the name of a musical instrument, and when "It" returns to the room, the players begin to make the motion required for any one of the instruments. One player gives the signal for changing the motions to that of some other instrument as often as he likes provided "It" does not see him give the signal. If "It" catches him giving the signal for the change, then he must become "It" and leave the room.

CHINESE CHECKERS

Number of players: Two to six.

Equipment: The board for this game can easily be made of beaver board, cardboard, three-ply, or, if desired, out of walnut, cherry, or pine. The game is played on a six-point star. Paint each point of the star a different color and then shellac the entire board. When six play, each has ten "men" in his point of the star. Men may be discs cut from old mop handles or half-inch dowels, sandpapered to a smooth finish and 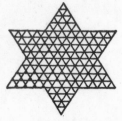 painted in the colors corresponding to those on the board. Or holes may be bored at the intersections and marbles or pegs used instead of discs.

Action: The men are placed on the intersections, beginning with the point, so that they are placed 1, 2, 3, 4, and so on. Each player tries to get his men across to the opposite star point. He may move in any direction except backward. Jumps may be

40

made of one man at a time as in checkers, but no man is removed from the board. Series of jumps may be made, of course. Often a player gets a "ladder" set up by which he jumps all the way across the board. No jumps or moves may be made back into an opponent's star point.

Three players can play the game using alternating star points for starting points. In this case fifteen men may be used.

FINGERS OUT
Number of players: Two.

Formation and action: The two players face each other. They count, "One, two, three!" On "three" they put out their right hands, either closed or with one or more fingers extended. At the same time they shout some number. The player who guesses the correct number of the sum total of fingers extended, or the nearest to it, scores a point. Five points may constitute a game.

TSOO! TSOO!
Number of players: Four or more.

Formation and action: One player is blindfolded. The remaining players are chickens. The blindfolded player says, "Tsoo! Tsoo!" meaning, "Come and seek your mother." The chickens run up and try to touch him without being caught. The player caught becomes the blindman.

FORCING THE CITY GATES
(Also the Philippines)
Number of players: Ten or more.

Formation: Two lines each with an equal number of players, ten to fifteen feet apart. Each team has a captain. Players in each line hold hands.

Action: A player runs out from one side and dashes with all his force against the hands of his opponents. If he breaks through, he takes back to his side the two players whose clasped hands he separated. If he fails to break through, he has to join his opponents. Then a player from the other side attempts to "force the gates." This continues until one side has no one left.

CAT AND MOUSE

Number of players: Ten to thirty.

Formation: Circle, with all but two players holding hands. One of those players is the cat, who stands outside the circle. The other is the mouse, who stands inside the circle.

Action: The circle of players revolves about the mouse. When it stops, the cat darts in at one side and the mouse goes out the other. The cat pursues the mouse, but he must follow exactly the path the mouse has taken, with no short cuts. The two wind in and out of the circle until the mouse is caught. Then two more players are chosen, or the cat may become the mouse and a new cat may be chosen.

LAME CHICKEN

Number of players: Two or more.

Equipment: Each of two players or of two teams has ten sticks, ten or twelve inches long. These sticks are arranged in a row about ten inches apart like rungs on a ladder, one row for each team.

Action: The player (lame chicken) must hop over these sticks without touching any of them. Touching a stick disqualifies him. After hopping over the last stick, still on one foot, he reaches down and picks up the stick. He then hops back over the remaining sticks. Dropping the stick, he hops over the nine remaining sticks, picks up the ninth stick, again hopping over the remaining sticks. This continues until all the sticks have been picked up. A player is disqualified if he touches both feet to the ground or if he touches a stick with his foot.

Variations: 1. The game may be run as a race. A player who fouls must start over.

2. It may be used as a relay. The first player hops over ten sticks, returning with the tenth. The second man hops over nine, the third hops over eight, and so on.

3. The lame chicken may change by hopping on the other foot every other round. The winner is the team with most players finishing without mistakes.

SHUTTLECOCK

This is an interesting game for all age groups. Many of the Chinese develop considerable skill in playing it.

Number of players: One to twenty.

Equipment: Shuttlecock, which may be made of four chicken feathers and a piece of thick cardboard. Cut out a circular piece of cardboard about an inch and a quarter in diameter. Paint it with cardboard or tempera paint. Attach the four feathers at the top center of the cardboard disc. Hold the feathers in place with a piece of cellophane glued to the cardboard disc.

Action: The player tosses the shuttlecock into the air and then kicks it with his foot back into the air. He continues this as long as he can do it without missing. When a player gets fairly skillful, he kicks the shuttlecock not only with his instep but with his heel, sometimes alternating the heel and the instep kicks.

FIST SLINGING, OR
FIST MATCHING[3]

Number of players: Two or more.

Action: One player acts as "caller." He wins or loses accordingly. He may take as many tries as has been determined, or the players may simply take turns. The caller calls out a number from zero to ten if two are playing. This call is made just as each player "throws his fist," holding up any number of fingers he desires. If the sum of the fingers on the two fists is the amount called, the caller wins. If it is not, he loses. Scores may be kept or penalties or awards made as agreed upon.

If three persons play, there will be three fists and therefore a possible total of fifteen fingers; for four, twenty fingers; and so on. The caller must call a number that will come within the total number of fingers that may be held up.

The caller may use names or other substitutes for actual numbers. For example, he may shout, "Tom, Dick, and Harry," meaning three; or "Romeo and Juliet," meaning two; or "double quartet" (eight); or "one week" (seven). The Chinese often call the names of places, lines of poetry, famous persons in history, and the like. This adds great subtlety and humor to the game, and calls for quick and witty thinking.

All calls must be made to synchronize exactly with the throwing of the fingers, so that no player can adjust his fingers in order to win.

Note the similarity of this game to "Spreading the Fist," page 47.

THROWING THE SQUARE

Number of players: Two or more, or two teams.

Equipment: Draw a rectangle, approximately twelve by twenty-

---

[3] The Chinese name means literally "throwing fists."

four inches, on the ground or floor. Divide it into two equal squares. Each player has a disc (a coin, a flat rock, or a washer).

Action: One player places his disc in one of the squares. The other player stands on a line about eight to ten feet away from the rectangle. From this point he tosses his disc at the squares. If it lands in the square with the other player's disc in it, he scores two points. If it lands in the vacant square, he scores one point. If it lands outside the rectangle, he scores nothing. Players take turns in tossing.

PICKUP RACE

Number of players: Two to eight. The game may be played by teams.

Equipment: One pair of chopsticks and two bowls for each player. These bowls are placed on tables or chairs eight to ten feet apart. Four or five marbles for each player. These marbles are placed in the bowls at one side of the room. For inexperienced players substitute marshmallows, popcorn, or nuts for the marbles.

Action: At the signal to go, players try to pick up the marbles and carry them to the other bowl. The one who first completes the four or five trips wins.

Rules: 1. The players must pick up the marbles one at a time.

2. Hands are not allowed to touch the marbles.

3. If a player drops a marble, he must pick it up, put it in the original bowl, and start again.

CLASPING FOR SEVEN

This game is so similar to "Buzz," "Counting to Thirty," and other such games that one wonders about its original source.

Number of players: Twenty to forty.

Formation: Players are seated in a circle.

Action: Players in the circle call out successive numbers, beginning with one. When it is the turn of one whose number is seven, or seventeen, or twenty-seven, or any number containing the digit seven, he clasps his hands instead of calling the number. These are called "bright" or "conspicuous" sevens.

Similarly on multiples of seven (fourteen, twenty-one, twenty-eight, and so on) the player should clasp his hands instead of calling the number. These multiples are called "dark" or "inconspicuous" sevens.

Whoever makes a mistake drops out of the game, and the numbering is begun again at one.

Other numbers, such as four, six, eight, nine, and so on, may be used instead of seven.

A more complicated version of the game requires the player to clasp his hands on sevens and multiples, smile at eights and multiples, and nod at nines and multiples.

CATCHING SEVEN PIECES

This is similar to our game of "Jacks."

Number of players: Two or more.

Formation: Players stand at a table or are seated on the ground or floor.

Equipment: Seven small cloth bags about one inch square. Fill with sand or rice.

Action: Players take turns. A player holds all seven pieces in his right hand. He drops them on the table (or ground), being careful to spread them out so that no two are touching. He picks one of the pieces up, tosses it in the air, quickly grabs another piece from the table, and then catches the one tossed into the air before it falls to the table. Similarly he grabs another from the table, until he holds all seven in his palm. He should retain the previous ones in his hand while throwing one up and grabbing the next one.

Letting the piece tossed into the air drop to the table or touching or moving the other pieces on the table except the one being grabbed forfeits the player's turn.

SPREADING THE FIST

Number of players: Six or more.

Formation: Players are grouped in teams of three each. Two of the three players form a horse thus: *A* stands erect. *B* bends his back, holding the hands of *A*, thus forming the horse. *C* is the "rider." Two teams face each other. Four players could play the game. In this case there would be just one horse.

D, the extra player, would stand in front of *A* and contend with *C*.

Action: The two "riders" engage in the game of spreading the fist. Each holds up his right fist simultaneously. As he does so, he calls a number. At the same time he holds up from one to five fingers. Whichever gets the correct total wins. If neither gets the right number, they try again immediately. This continues until one of them calls the correct total.

The winner takes *A*'s place in forming the horse. The loser takes *B*'s place, with bended back.

Arrange it so that each player gets an opportunity to be the "rider."

DA ERR

Number of players: Two or more.

Equipment: A stick about six inches long, sharpened at both ends so that, when it is hit on one end, it bounces into the air. Another stick, twenty-four to thirty-six inches long, is used as a club. A sawed-off broomstick makes ideal equipment because of its smoothness and durability.

A three-foot square is outlined on the ground. If teams are to play the game, the square should be smaller.

Action: The batter knocks the short stick into the air by hitting on one of its sharpened ends. While it is in the air, he hits it as far as possible with a swinging stroke. From the point where it stops the opposing player tries to toss the short stick into the three-foot square. If successful he becomes the batter.

Often the game is played with three or four players on a side. Each player on a side gets to hit the short stick. The first player hits from the square. The second hits from the point where it rests after the first player's smash. And so on until all the players on the team have hit it. Thus it is often far from the square after the last player has hit it. However, the team in the field gets one throw for each man on its team. By thus relaying it the last man is often close enough simply to drop the short stick in the square. That's the reason for making the square smaller when more than two play the game.

CHINESE HOPSCOTCH

Number of players: Two or more.

Equipment: Make a rectangle eight by four feet. Mark it into eight squares as indicated in the diagram. Each player supplies himself with a small, flat stone.

Action: Standing a few feet away from the rectangle, the first player tosses his stone, trying to land it in square number one. If successful he hops into square one and kicks the stone out of the rectangle. He then tries for square two. From there he must

4	5
3	6
2	7
1	8

kick his stone into square one and then out of the rectangle. So it goes until he has completed all eight squares.

If a player misses his throw by rolling or sliding out, or if the stone touches a line, or if he touches a line with his foot or lets the other foot down, he loses his turn.

If his throw is successful but he misses in kicking the stone out or he touches the other foot to the ground, he is privileged to put his stone in that square without tossing for it on his next turn.

CHINESE STICK RHYTHMS

Number of players: Two.

Equipment: Each has a stick six feet long (broomstick).

Action: Standing, facing, they make rhythm by striking sticks on ground, then striking them together. Positions: (A) On ground. (B) Sticks crossed high. (C) Crossed low. Right foot is forward, right hand in forward grasping position. Possible rhythms: AB, ABCB, AB, ABCB, and so on. Or go up to ten or twenty and back to two, as: AB, ABCB, ABCBCB, ABCBCBCB, and so forth.

BEACH LAME CHICKEN

This game is a good one for a sandy beach. In fact it is so used in China. Or it may be played in the yard or even in the parlor. It is very similar to "Lame Chicken."

Number of players: Two or more—or even one can have a lot of fun trying his skill.

Equipment: Usually bathing slippers are used. However, it may be played with bean bags, strips of seaweed, shells, or whatever is handy.

Formation and Action: Place five to ten bathing slippers in a straight row and about ten to twelve inches apart. There should be a row for each group playing. Each player in turn becomes a "lame chicken." He hops on one foot over each slipper. On hopping over the last slipper, he kicks it with the foot he's hopping on, picks it up, and hops back over the other slippers. After hopping over slipper number one, he kicks it, picks it up, and hops back over the remaining slippers. This process is continued without stopping until all the slippers have been picked up. During all this time he must never let the "lame foot" touch the ground. Nor must he touch a shoe except in regular turn when he is supposed to kick it and pick it up.

Players who fall, touch the "lame foot" to the ground, or touch any of the shoes out of turn drop out of the contest.

IAU CHHUNG

Number of players: Two to eight.

Equipment: Four sticks are needed for this ancient Chinese game. Two of these are of equal length and fat. The other two are light, usually of bamboo. They are about one foot and six inches long, respectively. The longer stick is the "club," while the shorter six-inch stick is the "twig."

Action: Lots are drawn to determine who will be first batter, second batter, third, and so on. The batter places the twig across the two parallel fat sticks so that it protrudes beyond them on one side. He sharply strikes this protruding end with a downward blow so that the twig rises in the air. The other players try to catch it as it comes down. If it is caught, the batter must take the field and the next batter comes up to strike. If it is not caught, the batter is ready for the next test.

This time the twig is laid crosswise on the two fat sticks, while one of the fielders throws the club at it. He has three tries from a position at least five yards away. If he hits the twig, the batter is out. If he misses, the batter takes the third test.

The fielder takes the twig and tosses it to the batter, who tries to hit it with the club. He is allowed three trials. If he hits the twig, it is allowed to fall to the ground unimpeded. The batter then measures the distance from where he is standing to the twig, using the club as a measuring rod.

A batter continues to bat until he is put out. Each time he goes through the three tests.

The scoring is by club measures. Each club measure is a point.

Fifty to one hundred points constitute a game, as decided by the players before beginning. The last player out is loser.

There are two penalties for losing—the "hmmmmmm" penalty and the hopping penalty. Before beginning the game the players decide how many times the loser shall pay the penalty— that is, whether it will be two, or three, or four times. The same number of times is given to each penalty.

To impose the "hmmmmmm" penalty, the winner tosses the twig as far as he can. The loser must run after it and bring it back, all the way saying "hmmmmmm." If he should stop saying "hmmmmmm" before returning, three more such penalties are levied.

In the hopping penalty the winner throws the twig and the loser hops after it, picks it up, and hops back without touching his foot to the ground. If he fails, three more hopping penalties are inflicted.

CATCHING THE DRAGON'S TAIL

Number of players: Ten or more.

Formation: All players stand in a line, their hands on one another's shoulders. The first person in line is the head of the dragon, and the last is the tail.

Action: The head tries to catch the tail by maneuvering the line around so that he can tag the end player. The line must not break. All the other players do their best to keep the head from catching the dragon's tail. When the head catches the tail, the end player becomes the head and the player who was in front of him becomes the tail.

FAN MIEN, OR REVERSES

Number of players: Two.

Equipment: A checkerboard. Sixty-four discs, each three fourths of an inch wide. These may be cut out of cardboard. They are one color on one side and another color on the other. Use paint or crayons.

Action: The play always starts at the center of the board, with the players alternating in placing the first discs on the four center squares. Then there will be two green and  two red discs at the center, if green and red are used. After that each player places his discs so as to capture some of the discs of his opponent. This is done by getting one or more of his discs between one's own. When this is done, all the discs in between are turned over to show the other color. Plays cannot be made just anywhere on the board, but must be made next to a disc already played. One loses his turn unless he can turn over one or more of an opponent's discs on his play.

The four corners are strategic points. Therefore skillful players try to maneuver opponents into making plays which give them the corners.

At the end of the game the player having the most of his color up wins. Placing a disc between two of an opponent's does not turn it over. Thus a player may place a green between two reds without penalty. But if a green is on one side of a row of reds and a player plays another green on the other side of the row, all the red discs in between the two greens are turned over with the green up.

If a player gets an opponent's man between his own men in more than one direction, diagonally, vertically, or horizontally, he turns over all men so caught.

WATER SPRITE

Number of players: Ten to thirty.

Formation: Two lines of players face one another twenty to sixty feet apart. Between the two lines stands the "Water Sprite," who is "It." The intervening space represents the river.

Action: The Water Sprite beckons to one of the players to leave the "bank" and cross the "river." Immediately the Water Sprite must close his eyes and count to ten. The player signaled in turn signals to a player on the opposite bank while the Water Sprite has his eyes covered. These two players try to exchange positions while the Water Sprite tries to tag one of them. If he succeeds, the person tagged takes his place.

KICK THE MARBLES

Number of players: Two, or more if desired.

Equipment: Two large marbles, an inch and a half in diameter, are needed. Two old golf balls or two tennis balls may be substituted for the marbles.

Action: One player begins the game by putting a marble on the ground and giving it a shove with his shoe. He then puts down the other marble and shoves it in the same way, trying to hit the first marble. If his opponent desires, he may call for him to kick the marble in a certain direction by ordering, "Kick east of the other marble." Or he may require that he kick west, or south, or north. If the kicker succeeds, he kicks again, trying to hit the marble. One point is scored if the kicker lands his marble east, west, south, or north of the other marble, as directed. A point is also scored for every hit. If he kicks in the direction ordered and hits in the same shot, he scores double the number of points.

FRYING VEGETABLES

This is a Chinese version of "Fruit Basket."

Number of players: Ten or more.

Formation: Players are seated in a circle, with "It" standing at center.

Action: All the players are given the names of vegetables— corn, cabbage, carrots, cauliflower, beans, beets, turnips, and so on. "It" calls the names of two vegetables. The players representing those vegetables must exchange seats. In the mix-up "It" tries to get a seat. The player left out is "It," and the game continues. If "It" calls, "Frying pan turn over!" all players must change seats.

C U B A

CHOCOLONGA

Number of players: Five or more.

Action: A player is selected from the crowd. He stands at arm's length before a circle or other marker on the wall. He is told to touch the circle as near the center as possible, while he is blindfolded. During the time he is being blindfolded and turned around three times, someone stands in front of the circle so that the player's finger goes into his mouth instead of touching the circle. This player catches the finger between his teeth and bites it gently. If preferred, some sort of pinching instrument may be used.

THE FLOWER GARDEN

Number of players: Ten or more.

Formation: Players are seated in a circle.

Action: The leader gives the name of a flower to each of the players. Then he says, "In a garden of flowers that I saw, nothing but the rose was lacking." Then he asks, "What was it that was lacking?" The rose answers immediately, "The violet was lacking." The violet must then respond, "The violet was there because I saw it. It was the pansy that was lacking." The game proceeds thus rapidly until some player fails to respond. This player must pay a forfeit.

THE NUTS

Number of players: Ten or more.

Formation: Players are seated in a circle.

Action: The leader gives such phrases as the following to certain of the players: "How many?" and "How expensive?" To the other players he gives numbers, five and multiples of five (ten, fifteen, twenty, twenty-five, thirty, and so on).

The leader begins by saying, "How many?" The person with that phrase must answer immediately, "Sir?" Then the leader says, "How many nuts did they give you at the store for a dime?" "How many" must answer with the number five or a multiple of five. The leader may either repeat the number or say, "How expensive?" or, "How cheap?" or any of the other phrases given the various players. Players must listen attentively and respond accordingly or pay a forfeit.

THE DOGS AND THE CHICKENS

Number of players: Eight or more.

Formation: Players are seated in a circle.

Action: Each player is given the name of a city or town. The leader starts the game by saying, "In ——— the dogs crow and the chickens bark." The player who has the name of the city called must reply quickly, "No, sir, in ——— the dogs do not crow and the chickens do not bark. Where the dogs crow and the chickens bark is in ————." The player bearing that name replies immediately in the same fashion. When a player fails to respond quickly or makes a mistake in responding, he must pay a forfeit.

THE PRIEST'S HAT

This is a Cuban version of "The Prince of Paris."

Number of players: Eight or more.

Formation: Players are seated in a circle. The person acting as leader stands at center.

Action: The leader says, "The priest has lost his hat, and they tell me that someone in this room found it and hid it. I do not know who it is, but I think it is ————." At the same time he points at someone in the circle. This player must not speak or smile, but with vigorous motions of the head must deny the charge, point out someone else, who in turn denies it and points to another person. The point of the game is to make some player laugh or smile, or to catch him off guard so that he fails to respond immediately. Guilty players must pay a forfeit. The looks of mock surprise on the faces of players charged with the offense and their solemn protests in pantomime are exceedingly funny. Before long a number of forfeits will be surrendered. When a player is guilty, the forfeit is paid and the leader starts the game again.

THE FANS, OR LOS ABANICOS

Formation: The players sit or stand in a circle.

Action: The first player says to the one on his right (in Cuba all plays are made to the right instead of the left), "My husband has come home from a journey." The second player asks, "What did he bring you?" The reply is, "A fan." The first player starts fanning with his left hand. The second player turns to the one on his right and repeats, "My husband has come home from a journey." The game proceeds this way until all the players are fanning with their left hands. On the second round each player continues to move his left hand in the motion of fanning and also his right hand, for the husband has brought two fans. If three and four fans are desired, both feet must be put into action. The last time around the circle the reply to the question "What did he bring you?" is "an image of St. Teresa," and the player bobs his head while both hands and both feet are going in fanning motion.

MY FRIEND HAS RETURNED FROM THE ORIENT

Action: Players divide into two groups. A line is drawn between them. One group decides on some object to represent in pantomime and then goes up to the other group and says, "My friend has returned from the Orient." The other group asks, "What did he bring with him?" The first group shows by pantomime. If one of the other group guesses what the object is, the entire group start running to catch as many of the first group as possible before they reach the "safe" line. Those captured they take to their side. The object is to get all the players on one side.

DONA ANA NO ESTA AQUI

The following song is sung by the players, in a circle, walking around slowly, holding hands, with one player in the center, representing Doña Ana.

Doñ-a An-a is not here; she's out a-mong her flow'rs; She's
o-pen-ing the rose-buds And clos-ing up the pinks.
Let's go a-round her house And see what we can see; They
say that Doñ-a An-a Eats par-sley and green peas.

Then Doña Ana sings alone:

> Who are these funny people
> That in my house do peep
> And neither night nor day
> Allow me to sleep?

The circle sings back:

> We are the jolly students
> Who've come to go to school
> And live here very near you
> In the chapel on the hill.

The circle stops, and the players ask, "How are you, Doña Ana?" Doña Ana replies that she has fever. The circle starts again, singing the first part, and then stops and asks again, "How is Doña Ana?" This time she replies that she has died, and her ghost rushes out and catches the fleeing players. The one she touches first becomes Doña Ana in the center of the circle, and the game is repeated as many times as desired.[4]

⁴ Spanish text and melody and game directions from *Canciones Populares* by Allena Luce, copyright 1921, 1949, by Silver Burdett Company, New York. Used with

CUBA AND SPAIN

This is a tag game the children love to play.

Formation: Players form two lines, opposite one another, about ten feet apart, or more if they want to run farther. One side is called Spain and the other side Cuba.

Action: A player from Spain is chosen to go to Cuba. All the Cuban players hold out their left hands, palms up. The Spanish representative rubs his right hand once over the palm of each player until he comes to the one he wants to run after him. Instead of rubbing, he strikes this player's palm; and the player chases him to his side. If he catches him before he gets "home," he takes him to Cuba's side and goes to Spain to repeat the performance. The object is to get all Spain's players on Cuba's side or vice versa.

SAN SERENI, OR ASI JUGABA PORQUE JUGUE

There are two variations of this game—the boys' and the girls'. In the boys' game there should be a leader, San Serení, who suggests the motions. At the words "And this is how they made them" all imitate the shoemaker or whatever other occupation has been chosen.

San Se-re-ní who lived a good life taught the boys to
Make good shoes And this is how they made them Tap tap-a tap-a tap.

permission. In Cuba almost all children's games are played with music, and this book has a number of them. The author calls them the Puerto Rican equivalent of Mother Goose rhymes. "Doña Ana No Está Aquí" is one of the more popular ones. It's similar to "Miss Jennia Jones," with different music. As the book is in Spanish, I have translated the words to fit the music as it is in the book.

Other occupations and their corresponding motions might
be as follows:

Taught the boys to drive a car,
And this is how they drove it (imitate turning steering wheel).
Taught the boys to paint a house (imitate painting with a brush).
Taught the boys to sing a song (sing tra-la-la-la-la-la).

The Spanish words are as follows:

San Serení
de la buena, buena vida,
hacen así, así los zapateros
así, así, así (Los imitan)
así me gusta a mí.

The girls' game consists of seven divisions of two stanzas
each. In the first stanza the participants, forming a circle, sing
their explanation of the fact that the child who is the subject
of their story was unable to go out for a good time ("pasear").
The group act out each duty as it is mentioned.

Monday morning early
A little girl went out to play,
But she could not play because
She had to wash the clothes.
And this is how she washed the clothes;
I saw her wash them so.

Tuesday morning early
A little girl went out to play,
But she could not play because
She had to starch the clothes.

61

And this is how she starched the clothes;
I saw her starch them so.

Wednesday morning early
A little girl went out to play,
But she could not play because
She had to hang the clothes.
And this is how she hung the clothes;
I saw her hang them so.

Thursday morning early
A little girl went out to play,
But she could not play because
She had to sprinkle the clothes.
And this is how she sprinkled the clothes;
I saw her sprinkle them so.

Friday morning early
A little girl went out to play,
But she could not play because
She had to iron the clothes.
And this is how she ironed the clothes;
I saw her iron them so.

Saturday morning early
A little girl went out to play,
But she could not play because
She had to clean the house.
And this is how she cleaned the house;
I saw her clean it so.

Sunday morning early
A little girl went out to play,
But she could not play because
She had to go to church.
And this is how she went to church;
I saw her go this way.

The Spanish words are as follows:
She had to wash on Monday:

> Lunes antes de almorzar
> una niña fué a pasear;
> ella no podía pasear
> porque tenía que lavar.
>
> Así lavaba así, así . . .
> Así lavaba así, así . . .
> Así lavaba así, así . . .
> Así lavaba que yo la vi.

Starch on Tuesday:

> Martes antes de almorzar
> una niña fué a pasear;
> ella no podía pasear
> porque tenía que almidonar
>
> Así almidonaba así, así . . .
> Así almidonaba así, así . . .
> Así almidonaba así, así . . .
> Así almidonaba que yo la vi.

Hang out the clothes on Wednesday:

> Miércoles antes de almorzar
> una niña fué a pasear;

ella no podía pasear
porque tenía que tender.

Así tendía así, así . . .
Así tendía así, así . . .
Así tendía así, así . . .
Así tendía que yo la vi.

Sprinkle clothes on Thursday:

Jueves antes de almorzar
una niña fué a pasear;
ella no podía pasear
porque tenía que rociar.

Así rociaba, así, así . . .
Así rociaba, así, así . . .
Así rociaba, así, así . . .
Así rociaba que yo la vi.

Iron on Friday:

Viernes antes de almorzar
una niña fué a pasear
ella no podía pasear
porque tenía que planchar.

Así planchaba así, así . . .
Así planchaba así, así . . .
Así planchaba así, así . . .
Así planchaba que yo la vi.

Clean on Saturday:

Sábado antes de almorzar
una niña fué a pasear

ella no podía pasear
porque tenía que limpiar.

Así limpiaba así, así . . .
Así limpiaba así, así . . .
Así limpiaba así, así . . .
Así limpiaba que yo la vi.

Pray on Sunday or go to church:

Domingo antes de almorzar
una niña fué a pasear
ella no quiso pasear,
porque ella quera orar.

Así oraba así, así . . .
Así oraba así, así . . .
Así oraba así, así . . .
Así oraba que yo la vi.[5]

LA MARISOLA

Formation: This game is played by a group of children in a circle, with Marisola in the center and one child outside the circle.

Action: The children in the circle walk around Marisola and sing:

Mari-sol-a was sit-ting In her flow-er gar-den Op-en-ing the rose-buds, clos-ing the car-na-tions.

With the last words each child in the circle catches hold of

[5] Spanish text and melody and game directions from *Canciones Populares* by Allena Luce, copyright, 1921, 1949, by Silver Burdett Company, New York. Used with permission.

Marisola's skirt. She protests in the singing of the second
stanza:

> Who are all these people
> Passing by my garden,
> Making so much noise
> That I cannot sleep?

Then the child who remains outside the circle sings:

> We are jolly students
> Come to spend our time
> In the little chapel
> Of our saint Pilar.

He walks around the circle, touching the head of each child
in the circle and singing:

> Handkerchief of pure gold,
> Handkerchief of silver,
> Come outside the circle
> When this touches you.

With the last word, "you," the child whose head he has just
touched leaves the circle. This process is repeated until Marisola
is left alone.

The Spanish words are as follows:

> Estaba la Marisola
> Sentad a en su vergel,
> Abriendo la rosa
> Y cerrando el clavel.

> ¿Quien son esa gente
> Que pasa por aqui?

Que de dia ni de noche
Me dejan dormir.

Somos los estudiantes
Que venimos a estudiar
A la capillita
De nuestra Pilar.

Panuelo de oro,
Panuelo de plata,
Que se quite, quite,
Esta prenda falsa.

MATANDILE, OR MATARILE, OR AMBOS A DOS

The words "Matandile" and "Mambroche" are nonsensical and cannot be translated.

In this game the player who represents Matandile stands facing the remainder of the group, at a distance of eight or ten feet, and sings:

A Mam-broche ha-tó Ma-tan-díl-e, díl-e, díl-e, A Mam-broche ha-tó Ma-tan-díl-e, díl-e, dó.

The others, in chorus, ask what he wishes:

What do you wish?
Matandile, dile, dile,
What do you wish?
Matandile, dile, dó.

Matandile replies that he is looking for a page:

> I wish a valet (or page),
> Matandile, dile, dile,
> I wish a valet (or page),
> Matandile, dile, dó.

The chorus asks what page he wishes:

> Which page do you wish?
> Matandile, dile, dile,
> Which page do you wish?
> Matandile, dile, dó.

Matandile in reply names one of the chorus:

> I wish ———— (name of player chosen),
> Matandile, dile, dile,
> I wish ———— (name of player chosen),
> Matandile, dile, dó.

The chorus asks what will be the trade of the child chosen:

> What trade will you teach him (or her)?
> Matandile, dile, dile,
> What trade will you teach him (or her)?
> Matandile, dile, dó.

In reply Matandile names a trade or a profession, such as laundress, cook, pianist, and so on:

> I shall make him (or her) ———— (the trade),
> Matandile, dile, dile,
> I shall make him (or her) ———— (the trade),
> Matandile, dile, dó.

The chorus replies that this trade or profession is or is not agreeable to the child chosen:

> That trade suits him (or her) fine,
>
> or
>
> That trade does not suit him (or her),
> Matandile, dile, dile,
> That trade suits him (or her) fine,
>
> or
>
> That trade does not suit him (or her),
> Matandile, dile, dó.

If the chorus says the trade is agreeable to the player chosen, he goes to the side of Matandile; and the above process is repeated in the selection of each of the other members of the chorus. If, on the other hand, the trade is not agreeable, Matandile suggests other trades, until the chorus says one is agreeable, and the player chosen goes to his side.

After the whole chorus has gone over to Matandile, they form a circle and sing:

> Let's go have a good time
> Jumping up and down.

The Spanish words to the song are as follows:

> A Mambroche bató
> Matandile, dile, dile
> A Mambroche bató
> Matandile, dile, dó.
>
> Qué quería usted?
> Matandile, dile, dile
> Qué quería usted?
> Matandile, dile, dó.

Yo quería un paje,
Matandile, dile, dile,
Yo quería un paje,
Matandile, dile, dó.

¿Que paje quería usted?
Matandile, dile, dile,
¿Que paje quería usted?
Matandile, dile, dó.

Yo quería a ———— (name of player chosen),
Matandile, dile, dile,
Yo quería a ———— (name of player chosen),
Matandile, dile, dó.

¿Qué oficio le va a poner?
Matandile, dile, dile,
¿Qué oficio le va a poner?
Matandile, dile, dó.

Le pondremos ———— (the trade),
Matandile, dile, dile,
Le pondremos ———— (the trade),
Matandile, dile, dó.

Ese oficio sí (no) le agrada,
Matandile, dile, dile,
Ese oficio sí (no) le agrada,
Matandile, dile, dó.

Celebremos la fiesta real
Dando vueltas en general.[6]

---

[6] Spanish text and melody and game directions from *Canciones Populares* by
Allena Luce, copyright, 1921, 1949, by Silver Burdett Company, New York. Used
with permission.

DENMARK

BIRD'S ALIVE

This game is similar to our "Jack's Alive."

Number of players: Six to thirty.

Formation: Players are seated in a circle.

Action: The players pass a lighted paper or stick from one to another. The player in whose hand the fire goes out must pay a forfeit, which he must redeem. (See section on forfeits, page 148.) Players may blow on the paper or stick to keep alive any spark of fire. As they pass the fire, they say, "Bird's alive!" [7]

BASTE THE BEAR
(Also Germany)

Number of players: Ten to thirty.

Formation: The players form a circle. The bear is seated on a stool at the center. With him is a keeper. These two hold to

[7] This game grew out of an old Danish tale of a nobleman who left a pet bird with a peasant while he was off to war. The bird died, and the peasant was punished for his negligence. As Danish children play the game, they say, "Lad ikke min Herre Fugl doee" ("Let not my Lord's bird die.")

either end of a piece of rope, about two feet in length and knotted at both ends to make it easier for them to hold onto it.

Action: Players move in to center and try to "baste" the bear (tag or push him) without being tagged in turn by the keeper or the bear. When a player is tagged, he must take the bear's place. The bear then becomes the keeper, and the keeper joins the group in the circle. At no time while the attack is being made may the keeper and the bear let go of the short rope. That means their range of activity is limited. In lieu of a rope they may be required to clasp hands, or a circle four or five feet in diameter may be drawn around them and the keeper must keep within those limits.

FISHING GAME

This is a Danish game, and tradition has it that it is played only at the Christmas season and that every child six years or under has a set of his own fishing poles.

Equipment: The poles are made from a thirty-six-inch dowel pin, cut in four lengths, making each pole about nine inches long. A small screw eye is placed in one end of the pin, a silken or heavy thread about seven inches long is tied into the screw eye, and on the other end of the thread a dress hook is tied. This makes the fishing pole. The poles may all be painted the same color or different colors, to add beauty to the game. The fish are

made from corks about an inch high or from rounds, about three fourths of an inch high, cut from broom or mop handles. Staples are driven into the top of the fish, and the fish are numbered from one to twenty on the bottoms, each fish bearing a number. The fish should be painted or varnished. They are placed on a table or on the floor for the game, not floated on water.

Action: Four players fish at once. The fishing is done by catching the dress hook on the end of the fishing pole into the staple on the fish. As soon as one fish is caught, he is unhooked and another is gone after. At the close of the game the player catching the *most pounds of fish* (as computed by the numbers on the bottoms) wins the game. The number of fish caught does not count. The fun comes when all players are after the last fish on the table.

STYKES

(Sticks)

This is similar to the Chinese game of "Iau Chhung."

Number of players: Five to ten.

Equipment: Two bricks or stones, a stick six to eight inches long, a stick thirty to thirty-six inches long.

Action: One player is batter. The other players locate themselves wherever they think he might possibly knock the stick. The two bricks or stones are placed about four or five inches apart, and the short stick is laid on top of them. The batter puts the long stick under the short one and gives it a boost into the air. The other players try to catch the short stick before it touches the ground. If they do so, the batter must place the long stick across the two bricks. The player who caught the stick then tosses it at the long stick trying to knock it off the bricks. If he does so, the batter loses his turn. If the short stick misses and hits the ground, the batter then defends the space between the two bricks with the long stick while one of the fielders tries to toss the short stick in between the two bricks. If the fielder is able to throw the short stick between the two bricks, the batter loses his turn. If, however, the batter fends off the short stick, he continues his play by placing the short stick across the two bricks. He then hoists it in the air with his batting stick and hits it as far as he can. Using his bat, he measures with his long stick to the point where the small stick landed. The number of stick lengths indicates his score. Then another batter takes his turn. This continues until all players have had a chance to bat. The game is played for two or three rounds, and the player with the highest score wins.

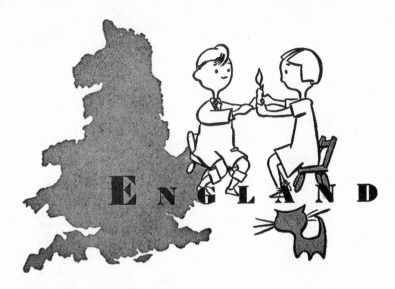

FOX IN THE HOLE

Number of players: Ten to twenty.

Formation: Players are seated in a circle.

Action: A lighted candle is passed around the circle. The player in whose hand it goes out must pay a forfeit for each offense. When enough forfeits have been collected, players must redeem them by performing certain stunts for the group (see section on forfeits, page 148). The candle should be in a candleholder to protect the clothes of the players from drippings.

HIT THE BUCKET
(Also Spain, Italy, Germany)

Number of players: Five or more.

Formation: Players form a semicircle around a bucket, standing at a distance of eight to twelve feet. Each player has a pebble, beanbag, or some other object to throw. Often a basketball or volleyball is used instead of a bucket.

Action: At the signal to throw, each player tosses his missile at the bucket. Those who miss must pay a forfeit, which they must redeem by performing some stunt (see section on forfeits, page 148).[8]

FOX AND GEESE
(Also many other European countries)

Number of players: Two.

Equipment: Thirty-three spots or holes are marked on sheets of paper or cardboard, or made in a wooden base or in the ground (see diagram). These holes or spots are connected by lines, along which moves are made. Seventeen counters (checkers, marbles, pebbles, linoleum or wooden discs) represent the geese, and the fox is represented by a counter distinguished from the geese by color, size, or material.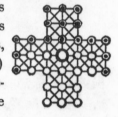

Formation: The geese are placed on every spot or hole in the three top rows and at the end of the fourth and fifth rows. The fox is placed on the center spot or hole.

Action: One player moves the fox and the other the geese. The fox has the first move. He tries to maneuver into such a position as to make it possible to jump the geese, as in checkers. Whenever he jumps a goose, he captures it and takes it off the board. He may jump forward and backward, up, down, and across. A jump is made possible when the fox is on a spot adjacent to a goose and the space next beyond the goose is vacant. The fox does not have to jump, but jumps only when he desires to do so.

---

[8] This game originated in ancient Europe. It grew out of a cruel game in which a pot with a hole in the bottom was placed over a chicken. The chicken's head protruded through the hole. A blindfolded player was given a stick, with which he tried to hit the chicken. Later it was played with a pot on a stick, which the blindfolded player tried to hit. It was called "Hit the Pot."

Players alternate moves, and each is forced to move each time. In other words, a player may not waive a move because it is not advantageous. The moves are made from one space to an adjacent vacant space on the line and in any direction desired.

The geese try to pen the fox so that he cannot move. The geese cannot jump. Only the fox has that privilege.

NINE MEN'S MORRIS

This ancient game is common to a number of countries. The French call it "Merilles"; the Germans call it "Muhl"; the English call it "Five-Penny Morris," "Nine-Men's or Nine-Penny Morris," depending on the number of counters used. It is mentioned in A Midsummer Night's Dream.

Number of players: Two.

Equipment: A board ten or twelve inches square. Three concentric squares are marked on this board, crossed by lines connecting the corners and in the middle of each side (see diagram). This makes twenty-four points or stations. These points may be drilled with a countersink. In this case marbles could be used for counters. 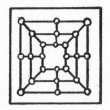 Each player has nine counters of contrasting color. These counters may be pegs (golf tees, for instance, marbles, pebbles, cardboard, wood, or buttons).

Action: The players place their nine counters, one at a time, alternately, trying to get three in a row. This is achieved by getting three consecutive counters on any line, except that the corner diagonal lines are not regarded as making a legitimate three-in-a-row.

When a player gets three in a row, he is privileged to take one of his opponent's counters off the board, except that he may not disturb an opponent's three-in-a-row.

After the counters are all placed, the players move their men, trying to set up a three-in-a-row. Each player takes his turn. Moves may be made only on the lines and for only one space. When a player is trimmed down to three men, he is privileged to move anywhere on the board, as he desires. Thus he may jump across the board to block his opponent and then move back to three-in-a-row on the next move.

The game is won when one's opponent has only two men left.

FRENCH BLINDMAN'S BUFF

This is played the same as our "Blindman's Buff" except that "It" has his hands tied behind his back instead of being blindfolded. This lessens the risk of accident and is great fun.

LAMARELLE

This game is played much the same as "Hopscotch." However, the French have some variations that make it a bit more difficult than the game we usually play. Note the diagrams of two of these variations.

Equipment: In addition to the diagram is a small flat stone or a disc made from linoleum or wood.

Action: The player tosses the disc toward Space 1. If it lands outside that space or on the line, he loses his turn. Spaces must be taken in their regular turn, except a penalty space, which he tries to avoid by skipping to the next space in order. The penalty spaces are "Start Over" in Variation One and Space 13 in Variation Two. In Variation One, when he lands at "Home," he can rest by putting both feet to the ground. Of course each time he finishes a turn, he can rest by putting both feet to the

ground before starting on a new turn. In Variation Two, if he lands on Space 13, he has to go back and start over. When he lands on Space 13, he rests before proceeding. He also rests before hopping over the remaining spaces.

DOG COLLAR

Number of players: Two or even teams.

Formation: Two players, on all fours, face each other. Their heads are in a loop of strong cloth. In some cases a belt is used for the loop. A line or marker separates the two players. Teams of players may be paired.

Action: At the signal to go opponents try to pull each other across the line separating them. At the end of one minute the winner is the one who has pulled his opponent on his side of the line.

BASTE THE BEAR

(Also Denmark)

Number of players: Ten to thirty.

Formation: The players form a circle around two of their number. One of these is the bear, who sits in the center of the circle. The other is the keeper, who guards the bear. These two hold onto a piece of rope about two feet in length, knotted at both ends to make it easier to hold. If no rope is available, the bear and the keeper may be required to clasp hands, the bear's right hand in the keeper's left. Or a small circle may be drawn around the two behind which the keeper may not go.

Action: When the keeper is ready he shouts, "The bear is free!" Then, and not until then, the other players may "baste" the bear. That is, they may tap him, strike him, push him. However, if anyone does this before the keeper announces that the bear is free, he takes the bear's place. He also takes the bear's place when the keeper or the bear tags him as he tries to baste the bear. The bear then becomes the keeper, and the former keeper takes his place in the circle.

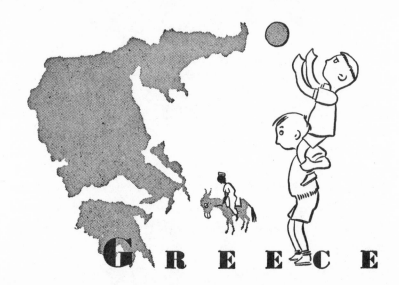

GREECE

PEBBLE CHASE

Number of players: Four to ten.

Formation: Players form in a line, facing a leader. They stand side by side, with their hands extended, palms together.

Action: The leader has a pebble or marble. He passes it down the line and pretends to drop it into each player's hands. He actually gives it to one of the players. That player dashes to a previously named spot and back, in order to return the pebble to the leader. The other players chase him. The one who catches him before he can return the pebble becomes the next leader. If the runner succeeds in getting back without being tagged, he becomes the next leader.

RIDER BALL

Number of players: Eight or more.

Equipment: A basketball, volleyball, or softball.

Formation: Players pair off in circle formation. One player in each pair sits on the shoulders of his teammate.

83

Action: One of the mounted players begins the game by tossing the ball to another mounted player in the circle. The ball is thrown from one to the other, no particular order being observed. If a mounted player drops the ball, he dismounts and changes places with the player on whose shoulders he has been seated.

ODD OR EVEN

This game was a favorite in ancient Greece and Rome.

Number of players: Two or more. If more, pair off. After each contest move on to a new opponent.

Equipment: A small number of beans (ten perhaps) for each player.

Action: One player puts some of his beans in one hand, closes it, and holds it out toward his opponent. "Odd or even?" he asks. The opponent looks at the clenched fist and guesses, "Even!" It happens to be odd as the player shows by opening his hand. "Give me one to make it even," he says; and the mistaken guesser hands over one bean. Now the other player guesses. On a correct guess the guesser is given one bean. This continues until one of the players has no more beans.

In a large group players go from one player to another. At the end of five minutes all players stop and count beans, and the one who has the most is the winner.

Variation: On a correct guess the guesser gets all the beans in the extended hand. On an incorrect guess the guesser surrenders as many beans as are in the extended hand.

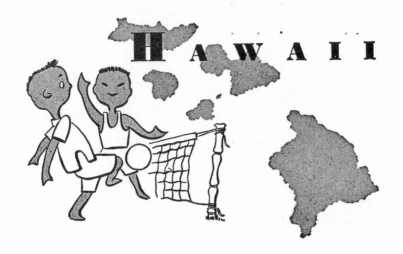

HAWAII

PAHEE

Number of players: Two or more.

Equipment: A short javelin, made of the hard wood of the "ulei" or "kauilor," is used. It is made thick at the forward end, or head, tapering off toward the tail end.

Action: The pahee, or javelin, is cast on the roadway or sward in such a way as to slide or skip along on the ground. One point is earned each time a player casts the pahee the farthest. Ten points win the game.

NOA

Number of players: Ten or more.

Formation: Two teams of equal number sit facing one another. Five piles of tapa (a bark cloth) are placed on a mat between the two teams. The piles of tapa are named in this order: Kihipuka, Pilimoe, Kau, Phihiluka, and Kihimoe. Under these piles the noa is hidden, beginning with the Kihipuka. The noa is a small piece of wood or stone.

Action: The teams take turns in hiding the noa. A skilled person acts as the hider for each team. He conceals the noa under one of the piles of tapa, faking as skillfully as possible so as to confuse the opposing team. The members of that team watch attentively while the noa is being hidden.

The following is recited by the man who is hiding the noa:

> Aia la, aia la,
> I ke Kau, i ke Pili, i ka Moe,
> Ilaila e ku ai ka noa a kaua, e Ku! [9]
>
> There it is; there it is;
> Under the kau, under the pili, under the moe,
> There is lodged our noa. It is lodged.

Now the watching side tries to guess under which pile of tapa the noa is hidden. If they guess correctly, they score one point.

The first team to score ten points wins.

PUHENEHENE, OR PA-POHENE

Number of players: Twelve to thirty.

Equipment: A long piece of tapa (a kind of bark cloth), made by stitching several pieces together. Sometimes it is called "Kapa," which means "beaten cloth." [10] The other piece of equipment is a pebble, which is called a "noa."

Formation: Two teams of equal number sit in lines facing one another.

[9] In pronouncing Hawaiian words each vowel is given its full value. In other words, it is pronounced as written.

[10] Patricia McHugh, of Honolulu, says she and her friends often use a substitute for tapa. They take regular brown wrapping paper and put an over-all Indian-looking design on it in shades of orange and brown. Then the paper is twisted and crushed until it is soft and wrinkled.

Action: One team has possession of the noa. A leader calls out, "Puheoheo!" and all the players answer, "Puheoheo!" [11] Then three players lift up the long tapa so as to make a curtain between the two teams. One player on the team who has the noa hides it on one of his teammates. The tapa is removed. All the players on the team with the noa lean forward and look down, to hide their expressions so they won't give away who has the noa. The other team guesses where it is, and if they guess correctly, they score one point. If they miss, the team with the noa scores a point. The first team to score ten points is victor. The teams take turns hiding the noa.

This game is usually played at night. In ancient times it was a favorite with adults.

LOULOU

Number of players: Two.

Action: The two players hook their right forefingers together. Then they pull. The player who holds on the longest without letting go or straightening his finger is winner.

[11] In ancient times the leader whistled the call on an instrument known as a "puheoheo." Then a player stood forth and chanted a gay and pleasing song. What this ceremony had to do with the playing of the game isn't clear.

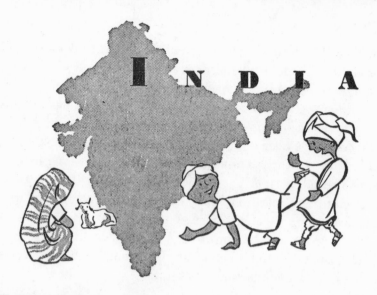

KABADDI [12] (Number 1)

This game is commonly known as "Hututo" in Bombay and in the central provinces. In Madras it is known as "Chedugudu."

Number of players: Ten or more.

Formation: Two equal teams stand on either side of a dividing line and twenty to thirty feet from that line. The line may be indicated by a rope or rocks or a lime marker.

Action: A player from Team One approaches and crosses the dividing line into Team Two's territory, calling out, "Kabaddi! Kabaddi! Kabaddi!" He goes as close as he can to the members of Team Two, trying to touch anyone of them with his hand or his foot and at the same time avoid being seized by him. If he succeeds in touching an opponent and in getting back across the dividing line without being seized, the player he has touched must drop out of the game. However, he must continue to call, "Kabaddi!" all the time he is trying to tag an opponent. To make it more difficult, this must all be

[12] This is pronounced "Kabad dee," with the accent on the last syllable.

done in one breath. If he is unsuccessful in his efforts and finds he is running out of breath, he must run back to his side of the line. If his opponents should seize him, he may struggle to get back to the dividing line. If he is successful in reaching it with either his hand or his foot, he is safe and the opponent who first seized him drops out of the game.

After a player on Team One has gone over into Team Two's territory and returns to his side or has been captured, a player from Team Two ventures into Team One's territory. The game continues until one side has no players left.

KABADDI (Number 2)

The Madras Olympic Association has worked out rules somewhat different and a bit more involved than the above simplified version. Some of these rules follow. They provide that the game be played by two teams of seven players each. A field fourteen by eleven yards is marked off (see diagram).

Players who are eliminated take their places behind the end line in the order in which they are eliminated and await substitution.

The attacking team is dubbed the "Raiders." The defending team is known as the "Antis." Teams take turn in attacking and defending.

The "Kabaddi" is known as the "Cant." In other words, the Raiders must keep saying, "Kabaddi," in one breath.

Scoring: If a Raider reaches home with Cant after touching one or more Antis, he scores one point for each Anti touched. The Antis touched are automatically out. They go into the end zone and await their turn for revival.

Each Raider must cross the Balk Line of the opposite team at least once during a raid. But in case of a pursuit the Raider pursuing and touching an Anti immediately following his raid need not cross the Balk Line and the Anti so touched is out. However, the Raiders must keep saying, "Kabaddi," until he reaches home.

An Anti, or intruder, if touched by one of his opponents with Cant, is out and the opposite team scores one point.

If a Raider is warned against any danger by one of his own team, the Antis score one point.

A Raider is not to be held by any part of his body other than his trunk or limbs. For any violation of this rule the opponent scores one point.

If a Raider succeeds in touching the March with any part of his body in spite of a struggle with the Antis, all those of the Antis who come in contact with him are put out and the raiding team scores as many points as the number of players put out.

When a team manages to put out the entire opposing team, they score two points in addition to the number of points scored by putting out individual players.

When only one or two players are left during any game and the captain of the team "declares" them out in order to bring in the full team, the opponents score as many points as there are players left before "declaring" as well as two points for putting out the entire team.

The whole side, when put out during play, is revived automatically and the opposite team scores two more points in addition to the usual points scored for putting out the individual members of the opposite team.

If a Raider who has been touched or held by one of the Antis

90

does not reach his home with Cant (that is, by continuing to say, "Kabaddi," in one breath), the Raider is out and the defending team scores one point.

Fouls: A player must not attempt to stifle a Raider's Cant by shutting his mouth, throttling, or any other way. The referee may disqualify a player for using such tactics.

Violent tackling leading to injuries to the body is forbidden. A player may be disqualified for breaking this rule.

In cases where a player is disqualified, a substitute may take his place. Each team is allowed a maximum of two substitutes. A team must not take over five seconds to send a Raider when asked to do so by the referee. Failure to do so is considered as delaying the game, and one point is conceded to the opponents.

Duration of game: The game consists of two thirty-minute periods with a five-minute rest between halves.

For junior and women's matches there are two twenty-minute periods with a five-minute rest between.

Other regulations: The team which wins the toss has the right to choose its home. The other team sends a Raider. Teams change homes for the second half of the game.

If the score is a tie at the end of the game, the game continues for periods of ten minutes each until the tie is broken.

"Time out" may be called by the captain of a team once during the first half and once during the second half of a game for rest or for substitution. Such "time-out" periods shall not exceed two minutes.

The Madras regulations require that all players be suitably numbered and all teams appear in distinctive uniforms. The numbers shall be six inches high and in bold type. Sleeveless jerseys with distinctive colors are suggested.

91

A Raider may become an intruder and may be put out by any Anti taking Cant when one or more intruders are in the raiding field. The team that puts him out scores one point.

By an intruder is meant:

1. A player found on the March or in the opponent's home when a raid is on.

2. A Raider who has left the March but is without a Cant, or a Raider who has lost his Cant before reaching home.

Exceptions: No Anti in a struggle will be deemed an intruder while the struggle is on. By a struggle is meant the holding of a Raider by one or more Antis to prevent him from reaching home with Cant.

SCORPION'S STING

Number of players: Four or more.

Formation: Players gather closely about one player, the scorpion, who walks on all fours. However, he is supposed to raise one leg, which represent's his stinger.

Action: The scorpion tries to touch a player with his raised leg. If he does, that player becomes the scorpion. The players tease the scorpion by touching his head, his shoulders, his hands, or even his stinger, being careful to prevent his stinging them.

KAE DANDA

Number of players: Five or more.

Formation: All but one player climb a low-branched tree, easily climbed. A stick two feet in length is placed on the ground against the tree. One player is the watchman. He stands at a distance of thirty yards or so from the tree.

Action: Anyone of the players may get down out of the tree.

The watchman tries to touch this player before he can get possession of the stick and toss it away. The player throws the stick as far as possible under his leg. When the stick is tossed away, the watchman must retrieve it, place it under the tree, and then try to tag the daring player before he can climb back into the tree. If a player is tagged before he can get rid of the stick or before he can ascend the tree, he becomes the new watchman.

If the watchman calls, "All jump!" all players must come down out of the tree. This means plenty of action.

KHO-KHO

Number of players: Eighteen.

Field: This is a team tag game with nine members on each team. The Kho-kho court is laid out as indicated in the diagram. It

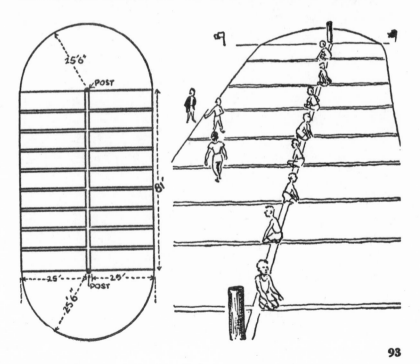

consists of a rectangular area eighty-one by fifty-one feet. At either end of the rectangle there is a semicircle with a radius of twenty-five feet, six inches. The rectangle is divided into halves by a central lane eighty-one feet long and one foot wide and in nine rectangular areas by marking eight lanes which are fifty-one feet long and one foot wide. These lanes are eight feet apart.

The one-foot squares in the middle of these lanes formed across the central lane are called "squares." In these the eight nonactive chasers squat (see diagram).

There are two posts at the ends of the rectangle, located in the middle, one at each end. These posts are made of wood and rise four feet above the ground. Their circumference should be from twelve to sixteen inches.

Formation: By toss it is decided which team shall be chasers and which runners. Eight of the chasers assume squatting positions in the squares. No two consecutive chasers face in the same direction. The ninth chaser takes his position at either of the posts to start the pursuit. Usually not more than two runners enter the court at any one time. When a runner is tagged, another enters the court to take his place, unless the ninth player is already in the court. At the start runners are permitted to stand or move anywhere, so long as they are within boundaries. Runners waiting to enter the court are seated on one side, out of bounds. They enter the court from that side only.

Action: "Kho" is the signal call in response to which a sitting player is to get up and pursue a runner. The call must be made loudly and distinctly. The chaser who calls, "Kho," must be immediately in back of the sitter, with his hand touching him. After the sitter gets up and joins in the pursuit, the chaser who called, "Kho," takes his place. Thus when a chaser wants relief, he calls, "Kho," and taps a teammate on the back.

No chaser is allowed to cross the lengthwise middle strip, although he is permitted to reach across the strip to touch a runner on the other side.

Other rules: Once a chaser starts in one direction, he may not turn to go back except at the turn post.

A runner is out in the following cases:

1. If he is touched by an active chaser with the hand.

2. If he touches any of the sitting chasers.

3. If he goes completely out of bounds. A player is not out of bounds if one foot is inside the boundary.

4. A runner is not out if a chaser committed a foul prior to his being touched.

A foul shall be called on a chaser if:

1. He changes the direction of his running.

2. He turns his shoulder line through more than a right angle.

3. He cries, "Kho," incorrectly.

4. He crosses the middle strip.

Each team alternates in chasing and being chased.

The maximum time allowed for each chase is seven minutes. There is a five-minute rest period before the other team takes the field as chasers.

Scoring: The chasers score ten times as many points as the number of runners put out. If all nine runners are knocked out before the expiration of seven minutes, thirty extra points are added to the score of the chasers and the game continues until the expiration of seven minutes. All extra players tagged in this additional time count ten points each.

SIA MAR DANDA

(Jackal Hit Wood)

Number of players: Three or more.

Formation: This game is played among trees easy to climb. Draw a small circle, eight to ten inches in diameter, under a tree. Place a short stick (danda) inside the circle. One player is selected to be "It."

Action: Start the game by having one of the players throw the stick under his leg as far as he can. This is the signal for all players to scramble. They climb the trees. "It" runs to get the stick. He brings it back and places it inside the circle. He then tries to tag one of the players. However, he can only tag when the stick is in the circle. Any player may get the stick and re-throw it, if he can do so without being tagged. The tagged player becomes "It," and the game continues.

GOOLI DANDA

This is similar to two Chinese games: Iau Chhung" and "Da Err."

Number of players: Ten to twenty.

Equipment: A gooli, which is a short stick about six inches long, sharpened at both ends. A danda, a stick about two feet long, used for hitting.

Formation: Players are divided into two teams. One team takes the field. The opposing team sends one player up to bat.

Action: The batter places the gooli crosswise over a narrow trench, made by digging a hole in the ground or by placing two bricks or stones an inch or so apart. He then hoists the gooli by placing the end of the danda underneath it and heaving it as far as possible. The field team tries to catch the gooli before it touches the ground. If it is caught, the batter is out. The field team then gets its chance to bat.

If the gooli is not caught, the batter lays the danda crossways near the trench. The fielder nearest the spot where the gooli landed tries to hit the danda by throwing the gooli at it. If he hits it or if the gooli lands within one danda length of the trench, the batter is out.

Otherwise the batter spins the gooli into the air by striking it on one of the sharpened ends with the danda. He then tries to hit it while it is in the air, knocking it as far as possible. He gets three such chances to knock the gooli as far from the trench as he can. After the final blow he estimates the number of danda lengths the gooli is from the trench. This is called the number of "lals." If not challenged, this is his score. If he is challenged, there is a measurement made. If his guess was too high, he gets no runs and is out.

Note: When I was a boy, in Louisville, Kentucky, we played a game we called "Dainty." It was very similar to "Gooli Danda." The game was very popular in the neighborhood where I lived. Boys up through the teen ages would find it a good game of skill today.

We used a broomstick to make the knocker and the "dainty." The knocker is from three to four feet in length. The dainty is about five inches long, sharpened like a pencil at both ends. The batter tips the dainty into the air by striking one end of it sharply. Then he tries to hit it before it touches the ground, knocking it as far as possible. When he hits it well, there is the same feeling of thrill that comes to a baseball player who hits a ball right "on the nose."

In "Dainty" a circle about ten inches in diameter is drawn. An opponent stands behind a line eight to ten feet from the circle. With an underhand toss he pitches the dainty at the circle. If he gets it completely in the circle, the batter is out and loses his turn. If any part of the dainty touches the circle, the batter gets one hit. If it lands outside the circle, the batter gets three hits. He then estimates the distance and calls the number of jumps he will give his opponent. If the opponent concedes, the batter scores as many points as the number of jumps called. If, however, the opponent accepts the challenge and jumps over the dainty in the number of jumps called or in less than the number called, the batter scores nothing.

Usually a score of 100 or 150 points is set before the game begins. The first player to make that number of points wins.

I have often wondered if the name "dainty" did not come from the Indian word "danda."

FOLLOW THROUGH TAG

Number of players: Ten to twenty.

Formation: Players form a circle, clasping hands and holding up arms to make arches. One player, the runner, stands inside the circle; and another, the chaser, stands outside.

Action: The chaser tries to catch the runner, but he must follow the exact route of the runner, going under the same arms. When he catches him or gives up, two more players are selected to be runner and chaser.

CHICKEN MARKET

Number of players: Six or more.

Formation: One player has charge of the market. Another is the buyer. The rest of the players are lined up in a row. They are the chickens. They stoop down and clasp their hands under their knees.

Action: The buyer comes up and asks, "Have you any

chickens?" "Yes, I have very nice chickens," answers the marketman. "Would you like to try them?" "If you please," responds the buyer. Then he goes behind the row of chickens. He places his hand on the first chicken's head and says, "This one is too tough." Then he puts his hand on the second chicken's head, saying, "This one is too old." He tries the third, saying, "This one is too skinny." At last he says, "This one is just right."

Then the buyer and the marketman take hold of this chicken, one by each arm, and swing it. "One, two, three!" they count as they swing. "You are a good little chicken. You kept your hands clasped, and you didn't laugh."

If a chicken unclasps his hands or laughs or smiles, he is put out of the game.

BALITO, OR LE BOCCE

(Also Croatia.)

Number of players: Two to six.

Equipment: Eight wooden balls, preferably of lignum vitae, four and one-half inches in diameter. Four of these balls should be marked with two rings so as to distinguish them from the other four.

An extra ball, three inches in diameter, is painted white. It is called the pallino or jack.

Field: The court or alley should measure sixty feet in length and eight feet in width. It should be walled by boards, two inches by twelve inches by ten or twelve feet in length. Joints of the board ends should be smooth on the inside of the alley. The backboards at the ends should be of the same construction but two and one-half feet high, with braced corners. All inside joints should be smooth. On the inside walls twelve feet from each

backboard a foul line is painted. A regulator peg is driven flush
to the ground midway of the backboards and midway of the
side walls.

The grounds should be as well built as a tennis court. At
each end the ground should rise for two feet to a point two
inches above the general level, at the backboard itself. This
keeps the balls from hugging the backboards. Along the length
the ground should have a slight pitch to the middle, so that rain
water will drain off easily. The ground should be smooth and
as hard-packed as possible.

Action: The object of the game is for each player to throw
his ball closest to the pallino and also to scatter from the pallino
the balls of his opponent.

One of the players, selected by tossing a coin, begins the game
by throwing the pallino, thus determining the bowling distance.
(The player to throw the pallino first may be determined by
having each player roll the pallino toward the regulator peg.
The one who lands nearest starts the game.)

When there are two players, each has four balls. The position
of the bowler is back of the twelve-foot foul line. The one who is
to throw the pallino bowls it any length he pleases. He then rolls
one of his balls, trying to land it near the pallino. His opponent
then tries to land one of his balls even closer. If he does not
succeed with his first ball, he rolls his second, third, or fourth
ball until he has the better position or until all his balls are
used. Then the first player takes a second turn and continues
until he has the better position or all his balls have been rolled.

The player having one or more balls nearest the pallino scores
as many points as he has balls closer than any of his opponent's
balls. If all four of his balls are closer to the pallino than any
of his opponent's balls, his score of four is doubled to eight.

When each side has a ball touching the pallino, or there is a tie, neither player scores and the pallino is thrown again by the player who threw it for that play.

The player who scores is the one to throw the pallino for the next play.

Twenty-one points constitute a game.

When more than two are playing, the players divide into teams. Each player plays his own ball or two balls apiece as the team may agree among themselves.

When three are playing, each throws one ball at the pallino. The one nearest plays alone and uses four balls. The other two take two balls each and are partners.

When five are playing, the two who comes nearest the pallino are teamed against the other three. The three decide among themselves who throws the extra ball.

Teams for match games number three each.

To dislodge an opponent, a player may toss the ball through the air in the effort to strike the opponent's ball on the fly.

It is legitimate also to hit the pallino and move it away from an opponent's ball.

Players may carom their shots off the side or backboards to get a favored position.

Variation: Use croquet balls on a smooth lawn with a golf ball or a toy wooden bowling ball for the pallino.

MORRA

This game is similar to the Chinese game "Fingers Out." It calls for the use of the fingers, vocal chords, and strategy.

Number of players: Two or more—no required number.

Action: Players pair off. There is no signal to start the game— just a simultaneous outstretching of the fingers of one hand.

102

Before the fingers are quite out, both players call a number between two and ten. If the number called by one of the contestants corresponds to the sum of the number of fingers extended by both contestants, a point is scored by the correct caller.

The game may be played by teams, with the players paired against one another. If there are four or less on a team, six points may constitute a game. With more than four players to a team, twelve points may decide the tilt.

JAPANESE TAG

Number of players: Four or more.

Action: The one who is "It" tries to tag a player. However, the tagged player must put one hand on the spot touched by the chaser, whether the back, the shoulder, the elbow, the knee, or other part of the body. In this position he must chase the other players. He is relieved of his position only when he tags another player.

When there is a large number of players, several taggers may be used at the same time.

HANETSUKI

This game is played a great deal at New Year's with gay battledore and shuttlecock. It is similar to "Badminton."

Number of players: Ten or more.

Equipment: Two shuttlecocks, which may be made of large

corks and chicken feathers. A tennis or badminton racket for each player.

Formation and action: Divide players into two equal groups. Each group forms a circle and is provided with a shuttlecock. At the signal to start, the shuttlecock is batted into the air in each circle. The group keeping its shuttlecock in the air the longest wins a point. The best three out of five may be declared champion.

Variation: Use a large toy balloon. In this case each side may have a balloon and proceed as with the shuttlecock, hitting the balloon with the open hand. Or a row of chairs may divide the two teams, and one balloon may be batted back and forth over the barrier. When the balloon touches the floor on one side, a point is scored by their opponents.

HANA, HANA, HANA, KUCHI

This game is similar to "Scrambled Anatomy."

Number of players: Two or more.

Formation and action: Divide into two sides, which sit facing one another. The captain for one side stands up and says, "Hana, hana, hana, kuchi," which means "nose, nose, nose, mouth." On the first three words he taps his nose, while on the fourth, instead of tapping his mouth, he touches some other feature, such as his ear, for instance. The idea of the game is for the players of the opposing side to do what the captain says and not what he does. All players who make mistakes may drop out or, as the Japanese play it, submit to being daubed on the cheek with flour and water.

The other captain now takes his turn. If the idea of eliminating is followed, the side with the player who stays in the game the longest wins. If the other plan is followed, the fun will con-

105

sist in artistically daubing the cheeks of the opposing players with flour paste.

The names of other features are "mimi" (ear) and "me" (eye).

It may be decided to play the game using only English. Thus the captain might say, "Nose, nose, nose, eye," at the same time touching his ear or mouth, to confuse the opponents.

Variation: The game may also be used as a circle game with no sides. In this case all players would follow the commands of the leader.

YEMARI, OR BOUNCE THE BALL

The word "Yemari" means "Handball," although the game is different from handball as we play it.

Number of players: Four or more.

Equipment: The ball is usually about two inches in diameter, or about the size of a tennis ball. Or a large rubber ball may be used, if desired.

Formation and action: The players stand in a circle. One player tosses the ball to the floor so that it will bounce straight up to him. As it rebounds, he strikes it back with his open hand. He continues this as long as the ball is within reach. However, he must not move from his place in the circle. When the ball moves near another player, then that player must bounce it and continue to do so as did the first player. The game continues until some player fails to hit the ball on the rebound. If a player misses, he drops out and the circle draws closer. This continues until only one player is left.

Variation: Each player bounces the ball until he misses, being allowed to move to any position to keep up with it. Count the number of times the ball is hit on the rebound. The highest score wins.

TAKARA-SAGASHI, OR HUNTING THE TREASURE

Number of players: Ten to twenty.

Formation: Two teams of equal numbers sit facing one another.

Action: One team has a coin (or other small article). They pass this coin from one teammate to the other (or pretend to do so) while the other team watches intently. The coin moves from fist to fist, with many gestures made to deceive the opponents. At a signal from the watchers all passing ceases, and the passers drop their clenched fists on their knees. The watchers ask the passers to open their fists, one at a time. The idea is to leave the fist holding the coin until all other fists have been opened. When the coin is uncovered, all fists closed at the time are counted and scored against the guessers.

Then the other side hides the coin, and the game continues. The side with the lowest score wins.

SCISSORS CHESS, OR HASAMI SHOGI

Number of players: Two.

Equipment: A board with 8, 9, or 10 squares on each side, thus making 64, 81, or 100 squares on the entire board (see diagram). The traditional board has nine on each side. A checkerboard may be used. Checkers may be used for counters, or marbles may be used if holes are countersunk in the board.

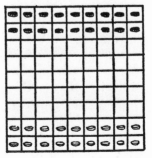

Counters should be of two contrasting colors. Thus one player uses red and the other yellow.

Action: The game may be played in either of two ways.

1. Each player has two rows of men at his end of the board. The object is to move his men so as to get five in a row not counting the two rows at his end of the board. Players move in turn. They may move as far as they like in a straight unimpeded line either horizontally or vertically. No diagonal moves are allowed. A player may not land on a spot already occupied, nor can he jump over intervening men, except that he can move up to an intervening man and then jump over him to the next space on the next move, if he desires.

When a player sandwiches one or more of his opponent's men between two of his own men, he has scissored him and he takes the opponent's men off the board. If he voluntarily moves a man between two of his opponent's men, that is not considered a scissors and the man remains on the board.

When a player gets five in a row, horizontally, vertically, or diagonally, he wins the game.

Men may be moved back and forth or sideways at any time to prevent capture or to set up a play, except that a player moves only on his regular turn.

2. Each player has one row of men at his end of the board. The object of the game is to capture and remove from the board his opponent's men.

Players move as in Game 1, no diagonal moves being allowed. They maneuver, trying to pinch an opponent between two of their men. No effort is made to get five in a row as in Game 1.

A man in a corner may be captured by blocking his movement. Occupying the two adjacent horizontal and vertical spaces accomplishes this.

FIVE EYES

Number of players: Two.

Equipment: Same as for "Scissors Chess" (page 107).

Action: Players hold counters in their hands and take turn about placing them on the board. The object of the game is to get five men in a row either vertically, horizontally, or diagonally. At the same time each player tries to prevent his opponent from getting five in a row. The first player to succeed is winner.

OKI CHOCHIN, CHRISSI CHOCHIA, OR BIG LANTERN, LITTLE LANTERN

Number of players: Three or more.

Formation: Players stand or sit in a circle.

Action: The leader calls, "Big lantern!" and at the same time indicates a small lantern by holding his outstretched hands close together. All the rest of the players must form a big lantern by holding their hands far apart. When the leader calls, "Little lantern!" he holds his hands far apart, thus forming a big lantern. The others must do exactly the opposite to what the leader does by forming a little lantern. Players who make mistakes may be required to pay a forfeit or may drop out until only one player is left. The leader tries to confuse players by always doing the opposite to the command.

KICK THE CAN

Number of players: Four or more.

Formation: A circle about four feet in diameter is drawn with chalk or lime. In the center of this circle is an empty can.

Action: One player is "It." The can is kicked out of the circle. "It" must retrieve it and place it back in the center of the circle. As soon as the can is kicked, all the other players run and hide.

109

"It" tries to find them. When he spies a player, he calls his name and dashes for the can. If he beats the hider to it, that person becomes a prisoner. If he does not, that player kicks the can and runs and hides again. Any hider may rush in and kick the can if he can beat "It" to it. The game continues until "It" has caught all the hiders. Then it may be replayed with the first player caught being "It."

SLAP HAND

(Also Korea)

Number of players: Two.

Action: This is a game requiring speed and alertness. The two players stand facing each other. One of the players extends one hand, palm up. The other player extends his hand, palm down, and gently strokes the extended palm of his opponent. Suddenly he makes a swift, sharp strike at the opponent's palm. The opponent endeavors to withdraw his hand so that the striker misses. If the striker slaps the extended palm, he scores a point. The players alternate in striking. A striker may feint at striking to keep his opponent guessing. However, if he makes a downward motion of striking, he is considered to have used up his turn.

JANKENPON, OR STONE, PAPER, SCISSORS

This game is like our "Eeny, Meeny, Miny, Mo." It is often used as a counting-out game to decide who is to be "It."

Number of players: Two or more.

Action: This game may be played in several ways.

1. Two players face each other with hands behind them. Together they say, "Jan-ken-pon!" On the syllable *pon* both players bring their hands forward to represent stone, paper,

or scissors. The stone is represented by a clenched fist; the paper by the open hand; the scissors by extending the index and middle fingers. The stone beats the scissors because it will dull them. The scissors beat the paper because they can cut it. The paper beats the stone because it can wrap it up. When a player loses, he extends one arm toward the winner, who "burns" the loser's wrist by hitting it a glancing blow with the first two fingers of his hand.

2. The game may be played by teams. They face one another in pairs. The leader counts, "One, two, three!" and on "three" the pairs contest, and one point is awarded for each win.

3. Teams decide on what they will do. All players represent the same thing. A mistake by any one player disqualifies his team and scores a point for the other side. Ten points is the game.

4. "Jankenpon Relay." The Japanese have a relay race built on this game. The course is square or rectangular in shape. It can be marked off by stones, sticks, trees, or chairs. Runners line up at opposite corners at the same end of the field. On the signal to go the first man on each team starts running around the square. When the two runners meet, they stop, put one hand behind them, and shout "Jankenpon!" On "pon" they hold out their hands, representing stone, paper, or scissors. The winner continues on his way. The loser drops out, shouting to his next teammate to start. The new man rushes out to meet the victorious opponent. Each time two runners meet, they stop to do "Jankenpon," the winner always proceeding around the square. The first team to get a runner to the opponent's corner wins.

RAKANSAN

Number of players: Six to thirty.
Formation: Circle, with players standing or seated.

Action: Players sing "Rakansan."

Ra-kan san ga so-ro-ta-ra ma-wa-so-ja-na-i-ka yoi-ya-sa, yoi-ya-sa, yoi-ya-sa.

As this song is sung, players assume poses of various sorts—hands up, finger on nose, hands held up in rabbit position, finger pointing, hands to sides of head, and so on. During the singing each player quickly assumes the pose of the player immediately to the right of him. A player who makes a mistake drops out of the circle for the next round. This continues until only one player is left. A player must be alert to note the original pose of the player to his right before the change is made.

FOREIGNER

This game is evidently an adaptation of "Sugar Loaf Town" or "What's Your Trade" as played in the United States.

Number of players: Any number.

Formation: Divide into two equal groups. These groups face one another, about twenty feet apart. The acting side is always the "foreign" group.

Action: The foreign group approaches to within five feet of the other group. "Here we come!" they call. "Where from?" asks the other line of players. A leader of the foreigners then replies, "America" (or Italy, England, India, China, Russia, Germany, or any other foreign country).

A leader from the home group asks, "What's your occupation?" The foreigners pantomime their occupation. They do it by wearing a cap and apron, kneading dough, baking bread, and so forth.

The home team tries to guess what the occupation is. When they guess correctly, the foreigners turn and run back to their country (indicated by a line or some markers). The home team chases them, and all foreigners who are captured must join the home team.

Then the home team becomes the foreigners, and the game continues. At the close of the game the side with the most players wins.

KARUTATORI

Number of players: Any number.

Equipment: Ninety-two cards. Forty-six of them have selected poems on them; the other forty-six have pictures suggested by the poems. These picture cards are displayed on the floor or table.

Formation: Players are seated in a circle.

Action: A leader reads aloud the poem on one of the cards. The players listen carefully. At the same time they look over the picture cards. As soon as a player thinks he has located the right picture for the particular poem being read, he snaps up the card. If he is right, he keeps the card. The player with the most cards at the end of the game wins.

If a player snaps up the wrong card, he may be penalized one point. This will prevent wild grabbing for cards.

Naturally the Japanese use Japanese poems. For English-speaking groups *Songs from the Land of Dawn,* by Kagawa and others (Friendship Press, 1949), and *Songs from the Slums,* by Kagawa (Abingdon Press, 1935), will offer a number of usable poems for this game. In the first book such poems by Kagawa as "O Skylarks, Teach Japan to Sing," "One with the Universe," "The Simple Life," and "I Call the Swallows" could be used. This book also has a section of selected classical Japanese poems. In *Songs from the Slums* poems like "Only a Flower," "If Only There Are Stars," "Autumn Sunshine," and "Discovery" could

113

be used. English and American poems like Leigh Hunt's "Abou Ben Adhem," Frank Stanton's "The World," Longfellow's "A Psalm of Life," Markham's "Outwitted" and "The Man with the Hoe," Kipling's "When Earth's Last Picture Is Painted," Browning's "Pippa Passes," are possibilities. Any good collection of poems will reveal others.

This is an excellent game for a youth or adult group. It can be adapted for children by using nursery rhymes and other children's poems.

POEM CARD PLAYING

Number of players: Four to eight.

Equipment: Two hundred cards. The poems used by the Japanese are those of "waka," or Japanese poems of thirty-one syllables. They are mostly lyrical poetry composed more than one thousand years ago. Each poem is divided into two parts by a pause. The first part consists of seventeen syllables and the second part fourteen. The first part is written on the first one hundred cards. The second part, or doublet, appears on the other one hundred.

Formation: Players sit on a mat, teams of an equal number facing one another.

Action: The doublet cards are dealt evenly to the two teams. The leader, or reciter, holds the other cards. Each team arranges its doublet cards on the mat where they can be seen by all the players.

The leader reads or recites the first part of one of the poems. The players, on hearing it, try to pick up the appropriate double card. A good player, on hearing the first few words or syllables of the poem calls to mind the second part. He locates the doublet. As soon as the first part is finished, his hand comes down swiftly with his forefinger touching the correct card. The first player to succeed gets the doublet card. At the end the team or individual with the most cards is declared winner.

This is a time-honored game among the literate classes. It is played by grownups as well as by teen-age boys and girls. It is played most often at the New Year season, at which time parties are given in the various homes. Besides being a good pastime it has done much toward popularizing poetry.

An English-speaking group would use poems or excerpts familiar to its people, such as Markham's "Outwitted," Kipling's "If —" Longfellow's "The Arrow and the Song," Holmes' "The Chambered Nautilus" (perhaps the last stanza, "Build thee more stately mansions"), Kilmer's "Trees," Carruth's "Each in His Own Tongue" (one stanza), Field's "Little Boy Blue." Any good collection of poems will furnish plenty of material.

Adapt the game to the ages and capacity of your group. With small children Mother Goose rhymes may be used. The number of poems and cards used can be cut to twenty or thirty. The player who gets the doublet reads it aloud to the others.

SUGOROKU

Number of players: Two to four.

Equipment: A cardboard or paper the size of a checkerboard and marked as indicated in diagram. The squares on the board lead to the center square or home. A wooden cube, one half to five eighths of an inch square, with numbers one to six on sides. Or a cardboard indicator with spinner. This can be made easily. Divide cardboard into six equal sections numbered one to six. Pin a cardboard arrow or metal spinner at center and flip it with the finger. Where it stops indicates the number of spaces to move. A small disc or marker for each player. A button will do. There should be a different color for each player. A flat space on the floor, ground, or table for the board.

Action: Players do "Jankenpon" (page 110) to decide who is to start the game. The winner tosses the cube or spins the indicator. The number he gets indicates the number of spaces he is to move his marker. If he lands on a square marked "sing a song," or "skip turn," or "move four," or some other direction, he acts accordingly. If he lands on "go back," he must begin all over again. If his throw takes him past "stop," he must stop there anyway. To land on "stop," however, means simply that he rests there until his next turn.

The first player to get his marker "home" wins.

KAGOME-KAGOME

Number of players: Three or more.

Formation: Circle with one player at center, who is the bird.

Action: The bird stands with his eyes closed. The others march around him intoning the following:

> The bird, the bird,
> The bird in a cage,
> When do you come
> Out of your cage?

After circling around the bird several times, they stop and ask, "Who is behind you?"

The bird answers, "Hanako," or some other name. If he is right, the person whose name he called becomes the bird and the game continues.

TAKARATORI

Number of players: Six to twenty, in two equal teams.

Formation: Draw a large letter *S* (see diagram) with a stick or line outdoors; indoors or on a concrete court use chalk. Place some heavy object, such as a stone, at either end of the *S*. This is the treasure or takara. Draw several islands around the *S*. Players of the two teams locate themselves about the letter.

One or more of the players for each team stand inside the *S* to protect the treasure and their team's end of the *S*.

Action: Other players locate themselves outside the *S* and venture in to try to capture the treasure belonging to their opponents. However, only when they are inside an island may they put both feet down. At all other times they must hop on one foot.

When a player tries to capture the treasure, he is tagged by an opposing player guarding the treasure. These two players then do "Jankenpon" (page 110). The loser is considered dead. He drops out of the game. All this time the players must stand or hop on one foot and can rest only by returning to one of the islands.

The first team to capture the treasure wins.

OTEDAMA

Number of players: Two or more, or one player can play alone just for the fun of developing his skill at the game.

Equipment: From three to six otedama (or beanbags). The Japanese make these out of colorful cloth.

Action: The game may be played two ways:

117

1. "Beanbag juggling": The player has two beanbags in his right hand. He tosses one of them in the air. Before it comes down, he tosses up the second beanbag, catching the first one as it descends. Before the second comes down, he tosses up the first again, and so on. This is repeated until the player misses. By practice a player can become rather skillful.

After developing skill in juggling two with one hand, add a third beanbag. Try the same thing by using both hands.

2. "Beanbag jacks": Drop five beanbags on the floor or ground. Pick up one of them, toss it into the air, and pick up one of the other beanbags before catching the one tossed into the air. Play just as in the game of "Jacks."

HANAKAGO

(The Flower Basket)

This is similar to "Fruit Basket."

Number of players: Ten to thirty.

Formation: Players are seated in a circle with one player, who is "It," standing at center. Cushions or chairs are used for seats. There must be a seat for each player except "It."

Action: Each player is given the name of a flower—cherry blossom, aster, and so on. "It" calls the names of any two flowers. The players representing those flowers must change seats. In the scramble "It" tries to get a seat. The player left out becomes "It," and the game continues. If "It" calls, "Hanakago!" all the players must change seats.

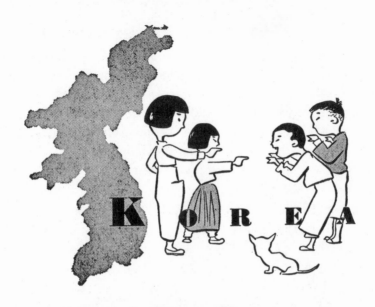

MAN, GUN, TIGER

This is an adaptation of the Japanese game "Jankenpon."

Number of players: Two or more.

Formation and action: Two sides line up facing one another. Each side decides which it will represent—either man, gun, or tiger. If man, the players hold their two forefingers up to their lips to represent a flowing mustache. If gun, the players aim, as if shooting, and yell, "Bang!" If tiger, they hold their hands up, claw fashion, and snarl, showing their teeth. The man beats the gun, because he shoots the gun. The gun beats the tiger, and the tiger beats the man. Score points.

WELL KONO

Number of players: Two.

Equipment: A board or paper about six or eight inches square marked as in the diagram. Countersink the five holes as in other marble games, such as "Chinese Checkers." Use four marbles, two of one color and two of another. Or mark the diagram on paper or cardboard, using a cork bottle stopper, the end dipped in ink, for the five spots. Make the

lines with ink, pencil, or crayon. Instead of using marbles, use checkers or cardboard discs, again two of one color and two of another.

Action: One player's men are placed in the two top spaces and the other's in the two bottom ones. The center spot is vacant. The player who has his men in the top spaces plays first by moving one of his men to the center. His opponent moves a man to the space vacated. Players move alternately. No jumping is allowed, and all moves must be along one of the marked lines from one space to the adjacent empty space. A player wins when he corners his opponent's men so that neither can be moved.

FOUR FIELD KONO

Number of players: Two.

Equipment: A board about seven inches by five inches with sixteen holes as indicated in the diagram. Or use cardboard and sixteen spots made with a cork stopper dipped in ink. If a board is used and the game is played with marbles, use molding around the outside of the board and provide a

space at either end for captured marbles. Sixteen counters (marbles or checkers) in two contrasting colors will be needed, eight for each player.

Action: Each player arranges his eight counters in the two rows at his end of the board. The object of the game is to capture all the opponent's men.

120

One player starts the game by jumping one of his own men so as to land in the next space beyond occupied by an opponent's man. By so doing he captures that man. Players take turns in moving vertically or horizontally, but never diagonally. After the initial moves of the game players move their men forward, or backward, or sideways, from one spot to an adjacent empty spot to get two men in such a position as to make a jump possible. A jump can be made only when a player has two of his own men together in adjacent spots, in which case he may jump one over the other to land in the adjacent space beyond, thus capturing the opponent's man in that space. A player does not have to jump unless he wishes to do so, nor can a jump be made except when it captures an opponent's man.

A man can be captured if he can be surrounded by his opponent's men so that he cannot move either horizontally or vertically. This is usually done by getting a man in a corner space with two opponents in adjacent spaces. Such a man is captured even though other moves on the board are possible.

YOOT

A missionary says this game is a great favorite in Korea, particularly at New Year's time. Adults as well as children play it.

Number of players: Two or more.

Equipment: A cardboard or paper diagram about eight by eight inches. The diagram is a circle or square of twenty spots. A cross of nine spots divides the circle into four equal segments. This cross is made by a center spot and two extra spots on each arm to complete the cross (see diagram). These spots may be made by dipping a cork in ink and printing on the cardboard or paper.

Four small discs, three fourths of an inch in diameter, for each player. These may be made of linoleum or heavy cardboard. Each player should have a set in a particular color—four reds, four greens, four blues, or four yellows, and so on.

Four yoot sticks, one set for each diagram in use. Since not more than four players can play on one diagram, it may be necessary to have several diagrams and thus several games going on at the same time. The yoot sticks are twigs split into two pieces, so that there is a flat side and a round side to each stick (see diagram). A convenient size would be two inches long by three fourths of an inch wide. The Koreans use twigs usually about a foot in length. Smooth the sticks by trimming and sandpapering. Paint or varnish them. This will add to the satisfaction of handling them. Excellent yoot sticks may be made of broomsticks.

Action: A player starts the game by tossing the four sticks up in the air. When they land on the table or floor, their meaning is as follows:

1. One flat side up, called "pig," move one spot.
2. Two flat sides up, called "dog," move two spots.
3. Three flat sides up, called "kuel," move three spots.
4. Four flat sides up, called "yoot," move five spots and get an extra throw.
5. No flat sides up, called "mo," move four spots and get an extra throw.

Players toss in turn and move a disc to the spot indicated. The object of the game is to get around the board and back to the starting point.

If a player lands a disc exactly on an intersection, he may move down that intersection, thus making it unnecessary to travel all the way around the board.

If a player lands on a spot occupied by an opponent, he captures that opponent and sends him back home.

Each player has four men to move around. He may exercise his own judgment about which one to move on a throw. The idea is to get all four men around. The one who does this first is winner.

CALAH PANJANG, OR BAMBOO LONG

Number of players: Twelve.

Formation: Players are divided into two teams of six each. One team runs while the other tries to catch them. The catchers must run only on the lines assigned them (see diagram). In other words, Number One protects his line, Number Two his, and so on. Number Six is in charge of the main line through the middle. The five lines are about twenty yards long and ten yards apart.

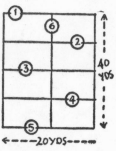

Action: At a given signal the players start running. The runners must watch their chance, keeping clear of lines where they may be caught. Chasers can run up and down only the lines assigned them.

If a player is tagged, the whole side is out and their opponents become the runners.

124

If anyone in the running group can run across the five lines and back again, he shouts, "Toe," to let the others know they have won.

BLIND GUESSER

Number of players: Six to twenty.

Action: One of the players is blindfolded. The other players pass by, performing some action. As they do so, the leader tells the blindfolded player what action each player is performing without naming the player. When every player has performed, the leader takes off the blindfold, names some action that has been performed, and asks that the guesser point to the player who performed it. If the guesser points to the right person, that person is blindfolded and the game continues. Otherwise he has to be blindfolded again.

TURTLE'S NEST

Number of players: Any number.

Formation: One player is the turtle, guarding the turtle's nest. The other players stand where they wish.

Action: Four or five pebbles become the turtle eggs. They are placed in a small circle, which represents the turtle's nest. The turtle stoops over the eggs, watching carefully. The other players slip up and try to take away the eggs. If a player is touched by the turtle as he tries to take the eggs, he becomes the turtle to guard the remaining eggs. This is continued until all the eggs have been taken. They are now hidden in several places. The last player who is the turtle has to search for the eggs. If he does not succeed in finding them all, he must pay a forfeit.

GRINDING STONE

Number of players: Any number.

Formation: One player stands beside the leader. The others stand about at random, but only a little way from the leader.

Action: The leader begins by saying, "Grinding stone! Grinding stone!" He then commands the other players to perform some action, such as, "Hop on one foot!" "Imitate a bird flying!" "Sing a song!" "Be the traffic cop at a busy corner!" The player standing beside the leader lunges after the other players trying to tag one of them before he can obey the leader's command. If he succeeds in catching someone, the player caught takes his place beside the leader.

LITTLE CLOWN

(El Lindo Payasito)

Number of players: Any number.

Action: The player chosen as Little Clown goes through some action of his own choosing, such as clapping his hands, stamping his feet, flopping his arms, and so on. The rest of the players mimic him as they sing or hum the following song:

Mrs. Temis Valderrana de Perez Rojo

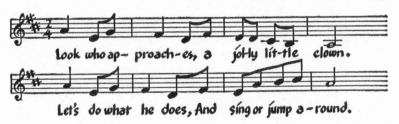

Look who ap- proach-es, a jolly lit-tle clown.

Let's do what he does, And sing or jump a-round.

Then another Little Clown is chosen, and the game continues.

127

THE LITTLE BALL, OR LA PELOTA

Number of players: Two or more.

Equipment: Mark a circle twelve to eighteen inches in diameter on the ground, sidewalk, or floor. Use a small ball (tennis ball, croquet ball, baseball, or rubber playball).

Action: One player is selected to start the game. He tries to roll the ball within the circle. While he is performing, the rest of the players sing the following song:

Mrs. Temis Valderrana de Perez Rojo

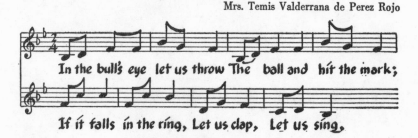

In the bull's eye let us throw The ball and hit the mark;

If it falls in the ring, Let us clap, Let us sing,

If the player is successful, the others sing:

> It has fallen in the ring;
> Let us clap, let us sing.
>
> Let us clap, let us sing;
> It has fallen in the ring.

If he fails, another player tries, and the game continues.
If sung in Spanish the words would be:

> En la rueda quiere yo, la pelota colocar
> Y si cae su lugar aplaudir y cantar.
>
> En la ruedo ya cayo aplaudir y cantar,
> Aplaudir y cantar en la ruedo ya cayo.

FRUITS

Number of players: Ten to twenty.

Formation: Players sit in a circle.

Action: One player is designated as master, another as servant, and the rest are given names of fruits—apples, apricots, bananas, blackberries, blueberries, currants, cantaloupes, dates, figs, grapes, guavas, lemons, loganberries, melons, oranges, peaches, pears, plums, raspberries, strawberries, and so on.

The game starts with the master asking the servant, "Where wert thou?" and continues as follows:

Servant: "In the house of the apple."
Apple: "It is not so."
Servant: "Then where wert thou?"
Apple: "In the house of the master."
Master: "It is not so."
Apple: "Then where were you?"
Master: "In the house of the plum."

So the questions and answers go. All players must use the words "thou" and "thee" except when addressing the master, when they use "you." Anyone breaking this rule or failing to answer immediately must pay a forfeit. The game is played until there are as many forfeits as desired.

COYOTE AND SHEEP

Number of players: Eight to twelve. One player is the shepherd, one the coyote, and the rest are sheep.

Formation: The sheep and shepherd form in a line, one behind the other, each with hands clasped around the waist of the player in front of him. The shepherd is at the head of the line.

Action: The coyote approaches, and the shepherd asks, "What does the coyote want?" The coyote answers, "I want fat meat!" The shepherd calls, "Then go to the end of the line where the fattest lambs are."

When the shepherd says this, the coyote breaks for the end of the line to tag one of the lambs. The shepherd defends his flock by extending his arms and running this way and that thus endeavoring to prevent the coyote from getting to the last sheep. The sheep and shepherd must not break their line. If they do, the shepherd becomes the next coyote, and the next man in line becomes the shepherd. The same thing is true when the coyote tags the last player in line.

ROMPIENDO LA PINATA

This is a popular game in Mexico, particularly at Christmastime.

Number of players: Ten or more.

Equipment: A large paper bag, the pinata, is filled with nuts and candy wrapped in wax paper. The mouth of the bag is tied, and the bag is hung from the ceiling (or a tree limb or door sill) with a cord. The bag is dressed and marked to represent a boy or a girl, using crepe or tissue paper or clothes.

Action: The players, each in turn, are given a stick; and with eyes blindfolded they try to break the pinata. They are turned around several times to make the feat more difficult. Only one stroke is allowed each player, and he is not permitted to grope for the bag. When someone finally breaks the pinata and the contents are scattered, all the players scramble for them.

Sometimes a bit of novelty is introduced into the game by preparing three pinatas—the first filled with flour and rice, the second with a pair of old shoes, the third with sweets, "dulces."

PERSIA

SOLEMN ACTION

Number of players: Six or more.

Formation: Players sit in a circle.

Action: One player is designated to start the game. He makes some motion, such as pinching the nose of the player to his right or tickling him under the chin. Each player, in turn, repeats this motion with the next player to the right. Thus it goes around the circle. No player must laugh or speak. If anyone does, he drops out of the game. The last one left is winner.

"HELP!"

Number of players: Four to ten.

Action: This is a tag game. The player who is to be "It" is determined in an interesting manner. One player stands with hand extended, palm down. The others place their index or forefinger on this extended palm. The player with the extended hand suddenly closes his fist. The player whose finger is caught becomes "It" and chases the others. If more than one player has his finger caught, the process is repeated with those caught until only one remains.

Those who are being chased may call for "Help!" any time. On such a call any other player may take hold of the hand of the calling player, thus saving him from being tagged. A player who is caught becomes "It," and the game proceeds.

CALABAZA

This game is similar to "Pussy Wants a Corner."

Number of players: Four or more.

Formation: Markers are placed about the room or yard, there being one less marker than the number of players. The markers may be made by chalk crosses or paper or flat stones. Players form a circle.

Action: Players sing in the same tone the word "Calabaza" ("everyone to his house") eight times. After the eighth Calabaza is sung, all players run for a marker. The player left out is "It." He then goes to one of the players and asks, "Are there any eggs?" "In the other corner," replies the player questioned. Meanwhile the other players are changing places while "It" tries to get a place. If he succeeds, the player left without a place must ask the question and seek to get a home.

BLIND HEN

Number of players: Ten or more.

Formation: Players stand in a circle, with one blindfolded player, representing the blind hen, at center.

Action: A player standing in the circle asks, "What have you lost?" The hen answers, "A thimble and a needle." The one in the circle then asks, "Where?" The hen replies, "In the haystack." The circle player then steps to the center and says, "Kneel down." He then turns the hen around several times. When he has finished, the players in the circle start running around shouting, "Blind hen!" until the hen tags one of them. The player tagged becomes the hen. Players may tease the hen by coming in close and shouting, "Blind hen!"

WOLF

Number of players: Six or more.

Formation: Circle, with one player at center.

Action: The player at center is the wolf. The other players call to him, "Wolf, Wolf, are you ready?" The wolf answers, "No, I've got to put my stockings on!" Again they call, and he answers, "No, I've got to put on my shoes." Each time he goes through the motions of putting on the piece of wearing apparel he names. It may be his hat, his coat, his pants, his shirt, skirt, or gloves, or whatever he chooses to name. Suddenly he answers, "Yes, I'm ready and here I come!" Immediately all players scatter and rush to a designated safety zone. It may be the bounds of the yard or the walls of the room. The wolf tries to tag a player before he reaches safety. If he does, that person becomes the wolf and the game continues. The wolf may get ready on any call that suits him.

PHILIPPINES

SAN PEDRO AND SAN PABLO

Number of players: Four or more.

Field: Outline a square at least ten by ten feet. Divide it into four equal squares by bisecting lines (see diagram). When more than four players are involved, enlarge the field accordingly.

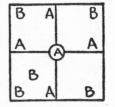

Formation: One player is captain for each team. On the defensive team the captain stands at center where the lines cross. He must always keep at least one foot in contact with this central spot. Four other defending players guard each of the four intersecting lines. No defending player may leave his line to tag an opponent. The attacking team scatters into the four squares.

Action: Attacking players try to cross the lines inside the field without being tagged. Each time an attacking player crosses an intersecting line, he scores a point for his team. When a player is tagged, he pays a forfeit or is declared out of the game until the teams change sides. Teams take turns being defenders and attackers. A defender must not step out of the outside line of the square. If he does, he is considered out.[13]

STOOP TAG

Number of players: Five or more.

Formation: Players scatter over the playing area with one player being "It."

Action: "It" chases the others, trying to tag one of them. A player may escape being tagged by stooping or squatting. However, each player may stoop only three times. After that he may escape being tagged only by running. Any player tagged becomes "It." In a large group there should be several taggers.

POTATO JOUST

Number of players: Two or more.

Formation: Two players face each other, about three feet apart. Each player must kneel and lift one leg from the floor. This leg he holds up with one of his hands. In the other hand he has a potato firmly jabbed on the prongs of a fork. A cushion may be provided each combatant.

Action: Each player tries to knock his opponent's potato off the fork, at the same time protecting his own. Players often develop quite a bit of skill in handling the fork—a slight turn of the wrist, a quick push, and a potato is flying.

A player is defeated if:

1. He loses his potato.

2. He topples over three times. (If he is obliged to let go of his foot in order to keep his balance, it is considered a fall.)

[13] Says Carol Moe, of Bayombong, P. I. "This game I saw first when children had marked out the lines with water on the dry beach at Aparri in bright moonlight. They were having a riot of a good time at it. I've seen it many other places since. . . . There are two teams of from two to five players each."

3. He stumbles against his opponent and causes him to fall.

Each time a fall occurs, each contestant is allowed to change the knee upon which he is resting.

LAME DUCK

Number of players: Four or more.

Formation: Players scatter about the playing space, with one player being the lame duck. Limits of the playing area should be determined before the game begins.

Action: The lame duck hops on one foot and tries to tag one of the other players. If he succeeds, the player caught becomes the lame duck and the game continues.

PUSS IN THE CIRCLE

Number of players: Four or more.

Formation: A circle four to six feet in diameter is marked on the ground or floor. A white string may be used to make this circle. One player, who is puss, stands in the center of the circle. The other players stand outside the circle, surrounding it.

Action: The object is for puss to tag the other players. They may be tagged whenever they put a foot inside the circle. They tease puss by stepping in and out of the circle or by feigning such action. Anyone whom puss touches becomes a prisoner and helps tag the others.

SIPA SIPA

(Also Hawaii)

Number of players: Ten or more.

Equipment: A hand-woven wicker ball, six inches in diameter. The court is twenty-five by fifty feet. There is a net three feet high across the middle of the court, dividing it into two twenty-five-foot areas.

Action: The rules reverse our volleyball rules in that the ball may not legally touch any part of the body above the waist. The ball must be batted with the knees or feet. In this fashion players try to bat it over the net into the opponent's court.

RUSSIA

GORELKI, WIDOWER, OR LAST COUPLE OUT

(Also Scotland, Sweden)

Number of players: Nine or more.

Formation: Players line up by couples. An extra player, who is "It," stands from six to ten feet in front of the head couple, face forward.

Action: When "It" shouts, "Last couple out!" that couple must leave the rear and move forward with the idea of passing "It" and taking hold of hands in front of him. They must come up on either side of the line of players and not on the same side. They may come swiftly or slowly as they desire. "It" may not turn his head to see them coming. He must look straight ahead. Only when they get even with him can he leave his place. When they do get even with him, he dashes after one of them, trying to tag him before they can join hands in front of him. If he succeeds, the player tagged take his place as "It" and he and the other member of the couple become the head couple. If the couple succeeds in getting together, they become the head couple and "It" tries again.

SCOTLAND

WEE BOLOGNA MAN

Number of players: Six or more.

Formation: A leader stands in front of the group of players, or he may stand in the center with the others forming a circle around him.

Action: The leader repeats:

> I'm the Wee Bologna Man;
> Always do the best you can
> To follow the Wee Bologna Man.

He then goes through the motions of playing some instrument in the band—a fife, a drum, a trombone, a violin, a piano, a trumpet, cymbals, a bass fiddle. Or he imitates an orchestra leader, a drum major, or goes through some other motion, as he chooses. The rest of the players follow suit.

A good leader puts the group through at a brisk pace. Each time he changes to another movement, he must repeat the rhyme.

Leaders may be changed often by the simple process of pointing or by calling the name of another player. The action should be fast.

HOW MANY MILES TO BABYLON?

This game originated from the practice of the toll charge that had to be paid when one entered a city.

Number of players: Eight or more.

Formation: Players stand, by couples, in two lines facing one another, with eight to ten feet between the lines. Couples hold hands.

Action: A dialogue takes place between the two lines, the players of each chanting their lines in unison. The tempo is fast. They sway back and forth in rhythm, swinging clasped hands by couples, as they sway and repeat the words.

First line: "How many miles to Babylon?"
Second line: "Only a bare threescore and ten."
First line: "Will we be there by candlelight?"
Second line: "Yes, you will, and back again."
First line: "Open your gates and let us through."
Second line: "Not without a beck and boo (bow),
Not without a side and sou."
First line: "Here's a beck and here's a boo,
Here's a side and here's a sou.
Open your gates and let us through."
Second line: "We'll open the gates and let them through."

At the words "Here's a beck and here's a boo" the players of the first line suit the action to the words by placing the hands on the hips for a "beck" and making a bow for a "boo." On "Here's a side and here's a sou" they stand erect and turn the head to the right and then to the left.

Then the partners clasp hands and run forward eight steps in rhythm. Each couple of the first line passes under the upraised arms of the opposite couple of the second line. Having taken the eight steps, the running couple turns around in four running steps, facing the "city gates" from the other side. The couples in the second line, the "gates," also turn in four running steps. Now the group is in position to repeat the game with the first line representing the "gates."

The game may be played to the music of "Country Gardens," if desired.

SMUGGLE THE GEG

Number of players: Eight or more.

Equipment: The "geg" may be a marble, a pebble, a knife, a key, or anything of the sort.

Field: A den four by six feet is marked off at the center of the playing space. Boundaries are decided.

Formation and action: Players are divided into two teams, the "Ins" and the "Outs." The Outs get the geg. They get into a huddle and hide the geg on one of their players. Or they stand in a line and pass it from hand to hand behind their backs, leaving it finally in the possession of one of their players.

The Ins stand by the den while the Outs, or "smugglers," run and hide themselves. Before they are finally hidden, the Outs must shout, "Smugglers!" The Ins then try to find and tag them. The object of the Ins is to find the player who has the geg. Since they probably do not know which player that is, they will have to challenge every player tagged.

If the custodian of the geg can return to the den without being tagged, the Outs win and they remain in possession of the geg for the next game.

When an In catches an Out, the latter is not a prisoner until the In takes off the Out's cap (if he is wearing one) and places the palm of his hand on the prisoner's head. When this is done, the Out must cease struggling. Then the In demands, "Deliver up the geg!" If the captured player has it, he must surrender it at once. The fact is then shouted aloud, and all players return to the den. If the player caught does not have the geg, he goes free. When the geg is found, the two teams change places.

URUGUAY

THE COLOR MARKET

Number of players: Ten to twenty-five.

Formation: Circle, with leader and two or three other players at center. The extra players at center represent artists, weavers, and/or decorators.

Action: Each player in the circle has been given the name of some color—red, yellow, blue, green, purple, orange, violet, black, white, brown, crimson, beige, chartreuse, tan, cream, gold, silver, gray, olive, pink, cerise, maroon, ebony, lilac, rose, and so on.

The players at center take turns in "visiting" the market. There is a knock. The leader or manager of the market asks, "Who is there?" The knocker answers, "Artist," or, "Weaver," or, "Decorator," according to whose turn it is. "What color do you want?" asks the leader. If he calls a color that is in the circle, the player representing that color leaves the circle and stands behind the buyer.

At the end the side having the most players wins.

THE BLIND HEN

Number of players: Ten or more.

Formation: Players form a circle with a blindfolded player, who is the blind hen, at the center.

Action: Players move in toward the blind hen, asking, "What have you lost, Little Hen?" The blind hen answers, "I lost my pencil and pen." The other players tease the blind hen, saying, "We know where they are, but we will not tell." The blind hen tries to tag someone before he can get back to the circle. The one who is caught becomes the blind hen, and the game continues.

THE WOLF

Number of players: Ten or more.

Formation: One player is chosen to be the wolf. He lives by himself, apart from the other players. Boundaries of the field are determined beforehand, and the "home" line is designated. The other players occupy this space between the home line and the wolf.

Action: The players frolic around the field (the space between the wolf and home base). They chant:

> In the fields let us play,
> While the wolf is away.

They then approach the wolf and ask, "Are you ready, Wolf?" The wolf answers, "I am getting up." So the others play in the field again. Each time they near the wolf and ask if he is ready. He continues to answer that he is getting ready. All of a sudden, however, he shouts, "I am starting to get you." With that he starts in pursuit. The player who is caught becomes the wolf, and the game is played again.

Note the similarity of this game to the "Wolf" game from Peru.

FORFEITS

In many games, particularly from Latin countries, forfeits are required of those players who commit some fault. In a small crowd effort is made to get at least one forfeit from each player. In a large group a game is continued until the desired number of persons have been caught.

The usual procedure in redeeming forfeits is as follows: A player is seated in a chair behind which is another person, who holds up the forfeits one at a time. The judge, or person seated, is not allowed to see the forfeits, although everyone else in the room does. The following dialogue takes place:

Forfeit holder: "Heavy, Heavy, hangs over your poor head." (He displays the article—a knife, for instance—over the head of the judge.)
Judge: "Fine or superfine?"
Forfeit holder: "Fine. What shall the owner do to redeem it?"

Then the judge pronounces the sentence by naming something the owner must do for the entertainment of the group.

If the forfeit holder answers, "Fine," the judge knows the article belongs to a boy. If he answers, "Superfine," he knows it belongs to a girl.

A list of forfeit stunts follows:

1. Repeat "Mary Had a Little Lamb" backward. The performer may be required to repeat all four lines or the first line in this fashion.

2. Imitate a fat man tying his shoelace.

3. Imitate a fat woman wearing a big hat getting on a crowded elevator.

4. Dance around the room three times with a broom for a partner.

5. Imitate a fat man getting off a crowded bus.

6. Bend your head as low as you can toward the floor.

7. Sing a popular song, with the crowd joining in on the chorus.

8. Repeat, "blue bread," rapidly five times.

9. Make faces in three different ways at three different people.

10. Smile three different ways at three different people.

11. Repeat rapidly three times, "Six sickly songsters sipping cider."

12. Imitate a girl on the phone talking to her best boy friend. Pantomime only.

13. Enter the room in three different manners.

14. Crow like a rooster.

15. Imitate the noise made by a cat in a midnight row.

16. Bark first like a small dog and then like a large one.

17. Quack like a duck.

18. Say rapidly three times, "Big black bear bit a big blue bug."

19. Balance a tennis ball on your nose. ("Three cheers for a good try.")

20. Imitate a cat lapping up a saucer of milk.

21. Be Sir Sad Sack, the knight of a rueful countenance. Select someone to serve as your squire. The two of you go to each girl in the room. The squire solemnly kisses the hand of each girl and then wipes the mouth of Sir Sad Sack with a handkerchief. The knight must look sad and forlorn throughout the ceremony.

22. Say three nice things about yourself while standing on one leg.

23. Imitate a gum-chewing, gossiping, primping typist in pantomime.

24. Spell your own last name backward.

25. Sing a lullaby to a sofa cushion.

26. Laugh five different ways.

27. Shake hands with five different people in five different kinds of handshakes.

28. Pantomime a saleslady trying to sell a hat to a hard-to-please lady customer.

29. Pantomime a baseball pitcher in the act of pitching to a batter and then catching the pop fly which the batter hits near the pitcher's box.

30. Pantomime a baby sitter taking care of a squalling baby.

31. Say rapidly three times, "Shoes and socks shocked Susan."

32. Say rapidly three times, "Sam sawed six slick, slim, slender saplings."

33. Put one hand where the other hand cannot touch it. This is done by putting one hand on the elbow, back of the wrist, or forearm of the other arm. (Let the victim try to work it out for himself.)

34. Place an object in the room on the floor so that no one can jump over it. This is done by placing the object in a corner against the wall.

35. Imitate a girl dressing her hair before a mirror.

36. Repeat dramatically Hamlet's line, "To be, or not to be: that is the question."

37. Hold an imaginary conversation with some noted historical character (Christopher Columbus, George Washington, Abraham Lincoln, and so on).

38. Pose as the Statue of Liberty.

39. Pantomime the teaching of a class in geography.

40. Deliver a half-minute Fourth-of-July oration.

41. Pantomime anger, grief, remorse, joy, hatred, love, ecstasy.

42. Imitate a farmer calling hogs.

43. Pantomime a person driving a jeep over a very rough road.

44. Pantomime both the photographer and the person whose picture is being taken. Try to get the subject to smile. As the subject do your best to display your "ivories."

45. Pantomime a rooter at a football game. An important goal after touchdown is being kicked. You want it to be good. The ball is snapped. It is kicked. It is in the air. It just goes over the crossbar for a successful kick. Whew!

46. Repeat in dramatic manner, "Give me liberty, or give me death!"

47. Pick three other people in the room to help you sing a quartet selection.

48. Give three reasons why we ought to let you go on living.

49. Pantomime a boy (girl) ordering an ice-cream soda and consuming it on a hot summer day. Place your order, receive it, get a straw, and go to work.

50. Deliver a dramatic speech, repeating only the letters of the alphabet.

51. Pantomime "Little Miss Muffet" when the spider sat down beside her.

52. Pantomime "Little Jack Horner."

53. Pantomime a basketball player shooting a foul.

54. Pantomime a boy flying a kite.

55. Pantomime a dentist who is pulling a tooth hard to get. Use someone in the group as your patient.

56. Pantomime someone with a bad case of mumps.

57. Pantomime a girl unwillingly washing dishes.

58. Repeat three times the following, "Seven simple sleepy sailors slipping sideways in sleet and slush."

GAME INDEX

A

African Blindman's Buff, 15-16
African Game Trap, 18
African Handball, 17
African Simon Says, 17-18
Ambos a Dos (*Cuba*), 67-70
Arches, African variation of, 18
Arrow Game (*American Indian*), 24
Asi Jugaba Porque Jugue (*Cuba*), 60-65

B

Badminton, variations of, 26, 104-5
Balito (*Italy*), 100-102
Ball Race (*American Indian*), 22
Bamboo Long (*Malaya*), 124-25
Baste the Bear (*Denmark*), 71-72
Baste the Bear (*Germany*), 81-82
Battledore and Shuttlecock (*American Indian*), 26
Beach Lame Chicken (*China*), 49-50
Beanbag jacks (*Japan*), 118
Beanbag juggling (*Japan*), 118
Big Lantern, Little Lantern (*Japan*), 109
Bird's Alive (*Denmark*), 71
Blind Guesser (*Malaya*), 125
Blind Hen (*Peru*), 133
Blind Hen, The (*Uruguay*), 146

Bounce the Ball (*Japan*), 106-7
Buckskin Ball (*American Indian*), 24-25
Bull in the Ring, African variation of, 16-17
Buzz, Chinese variation of, 45-46

C

Calabaza (*Peru*), 132-33
Calah Panjang (*Malaya*), 124-25
Cambio de Instrumentos (*Chile*), 39
Cat and Mouse (*China*), 42
Cat and Rat (*Brazil*), 30-31
Catching Seven Pieces (*China*), 46-47
Catching the Dragon's Tail (*China*), 51-52
Cattle Stockade (*Africa*), 16-17
Chedugudu (*Madras*), 88-89
Chicken Market (*Italy*), 99-100
Chinese Checkers, 40-41
Chinese Hopscotch, 48-49
Chinese Stick Rhythms, 49
Chocolonga (*Cuba*), 55
Clasping for Seven (*China*), 45-46
Color Market, The (*Uruguay*), 145
Coyote and Sheep (*Mexico*), 129-30
Cuba and Spain (*Cuba*), 60

D

Da Err (*China*), 47-48
Dainty, 97-98
Diviyan Keliya (*Ceylon*), 34-35
Dog Collar (*Germany*), 81
Dogs and the Chickens, The (*Cuba*), 56-57
Dona Ana No Esta Aqui (*Cuba*), 58-59

E

Eagle and the Pigeon (*Bolivia*), 28-29
Eeny, Meeny, Miny, Mo, variations of, 110-11, 119
El Lindo Payasito (*Mexico*), 127
Eskimo Escapades (*Alaska*), 20-21

F

Fan Mien (*China*), 52-53
Fans, The (*Cuba*), 57-58
Fingers Out (*China*), 41
Fishing Game (*Denmark*), 72-73
Fist Matching (*China*), 44
Fist Slinging (*China*), 44
Five Eyes (*Japan*), 109
Five-Penny Morris (*England*), 77-78
Flower Basket, The (*Japan*), 118
Flower Garden, The (*Cuba*), 55-56
Follow Through Tag (*Italy*), 99
Forcing the City Gates (*China*), 41-42
Foreigner (*Japan*), 112-13
Four Field Kono (*Korea*), 120-21
Fox and Geese, Ceylonese variation of, 34-35
Fox and Geese (*England*), 76-77
Fox in the Hole (*England*), 75
French Blindman's Buff, 79
Fruit Basket, variations of, 38, 54, 118
Fruits (*Mexico*), 129
Frying Vegetables (*China*), 54

G

Gooli Danda (*India*), 96-98
Gorelki (*Russia*), 139
Grab Bag (*Brazil*), 32
Grinding Stone (*Malaya*), 126

H

Hana, Hana, Hana, Kuchi (*Japan*), 105-6
Hanakago (*Japan*), 118
Handball, Japanese variation of, 106-7
Handkerchief game (*Bolivia*), 27
Hanetsuki (*Japan*), 104-5
Hasami Shogi (*Japan*), 107-8
"Help!" (*Peru*), 132
Hen and Wildcat (*Africa*), 16
Hit the Bucket (*England*), 75-76
Hit the Penny (*Brazil*), 31
Hit the Pot (*Europe*), 76
Hopscotch, variations of, 48-49, 79-80
How Many Miles to Babylon? (*Scotland*), 142-43
Hunting the Treasure (*Japan*), 107
Hututo (*Bombay*), 88-89

I

Iau Chhung (*China*), 50-51

J

Jackal Hit Wood (*India*), 95-96
Jacks, variations of, 46-47, 118
Jankenpon (*Japan*), 110-11
Jankenpon Relay (*Japan*), 111
Japanese Tag, 104
Jarabadach (*Africa*), 18-19
Juego del Panuelo (*Bolivia*), 27

K

Kabaddi, No. 1 (*India*), 88-89
Kabaddi, No. 2 (*India*), 89-92
Kae Danda (*India*), 92-93
Kogome-Kogome (*Japan*), 116
Karutatori (*Japan*), 113-14
Kho-Kho (*India*), 93-95
Kick the Can (*Japan*), 109-10
Kick the Marbles (*China*), 53-54
Kick the Stick Relay (*American Indian*), 26
King's Messenger, The (*Chile*), 37

L

La Barra (*Chile*), 36
La Canasta (*Chile*), 38

La Marisola (*Cuba*), 65-67
La Palma (*Bolivia*), 28-29
La Pelota (*Mexico*), 128
LaMarelle (*France*), 79-80
Lame Chicken (*China*), 42-43
Lame Duck (*Philippines*), 137
Last Couple Out (*Russia*), 139-40
Le Bocce (*Italy*), 100-102
Leopards and Cattle (*Ceylon*), 34-35
Lion and Deer Tag (*Africa*), 17
Little Ball, The (*Mexico*), 128
Little Clown (*Mexico*), 127
Loo K'bah Zee (*Burma*), 33
Los Abanicos (*Cuba*), 57-58
Loulou (*Hawaii*), 87

M

Man, Gun, Tiger (*Korea*), 119
Matandile (*Cuba*), 67-70
Matarile (*Cuba*), 67-70
Merilles (*France*), 77-78
Morra (*Italy*), 102-3
Morral (*Brazil*), 32
Muhl (*Germany*), 77-78
Mulambilwa (*Africa*), 15
My Friend Has Returned from the Orient (*Cuba*), 58

N

Nine Men's Morris (*England*), 77-78
Nine-Penny Morris (*England*), 77-78
Noa (*Hawaii*), 85-86
Nsikwi (*Africa*), 16
Nuts, The (*Cuba*), 56

O

Odd or Even (*Greece*), 84
Oki Chochin Chrissi Chochia (*Japan*), 109
Otedama (*Japan*), 117-18

P

Pa-Pohene (*Hawaii*), 86-87
Pahee (*Hawaii*), 85
Paloma y Gavilan (*Bolivia*), 28
Papago (*American Indian*), 25
Pebble Chase (*Greece*), 83
Pickup Race (*China*), 45

Pima Sticks (*American Indian*), 23-24
Poem Card Playing (*Japan*), 114-15
Potato Joust (*Philippines*), 136-37
Priest's Hat, The (*Cuba*), 57
Prince of Paris, The, Cuban variation of, 57
Puhenehene (*Hawaii*), 86-87
Puss in the Circle (*Philippines*), 137
Pussy Wants a Corner, Peruvian variation of, 132-33

R

Rakansan (*Japan*), 111-12
Reverses (*China*), 52-53
Rider Ball (*Greece*), 83-84
Ring and Arrow (*American Indian*), 25-26
Rompiendo la Pinata (*Mexico*), 130

S

San Pedro and San Pablo (*Philippines*), 135-36
San Sereni (*Cuba*), 60-65
Scissors Chess (*Japan*), 107-8
Scorpion's Sting (*India*), 92
Scrambled Anatomy, Japanese variation of, 105-6
Shuttlecock (*China*), 43
Sia Mar Danda (*India*), 95-96
Sipa Sipa (*Philippines*), 137-38
Slap Hand (*Japan*), 110
Smuggle the Geg (*Scotland*), 143-44
Solemn Action (*Persia*), 131
Spear the Whale (*Alaska*), 20-21
Spreading the Fist (*China*), 47
Sticks (*Denmark*), 73-74
Stone, Paper, Scissors (*Japan*), 110-11
Stoop Tag (*Philippines*), 136
Stykes (*Denmark*), 73-74
Sugoroku (*Japan*), 115-16

T

Takara-Sagashi (*Japan*), 107
Takaratori (*Japan*), 117
Throwing the Square (*China*), 44-45
Ticktacktoe, African variation of, 18-19
Tokinawas (*American Indian*), 25-26
Tsoo! Tsoo! (*China*), 41
Turtle's Nest (*Malaya*), 125

V

Va El Tren (*Chile*), 37-38
Volleyball, Filipino variation of, 137-38

W

Water Sprite (*China*), 53
Wee Bologna Man (*Scotland*), 141-42
Well Kono (*Korea*), 119-20

Where Is the Stick? (*American Indian*), 22-23
Widower (*Scotland*), 139-40
Wolf (*Peru*), 133-34
Wolf, The (*Uruguay*), 146-47

Y

Yemari (*Japan*), 106-7
Yoot (*Korea*), 121-23

CLASSIFIED INDEX

Ball Games

African Handball, 17
Balito, 100-102
Ball Race, 22
Buckskin Ball, 24-25
Mulambilwa, 15
Nsikwi, 16
Rider Ball, 83-84
Sipa Sipa, 137-38
Yemari, 106-7

Batting Games

Da Err, 47-48
Gooli Danda, 96-98
Iau Chhung, 50-51
Stykes, 73-74

Blindfold Games

African Blindman's Buff, 15-16
Blind Guesser, 125
Blind Hen, 133
Blind Hen, The, 146
Chocolonga, 55
French Blindman's Buff, 79
Rompiendo la Pinata, 130
Tsoo! Tsoo! 41

Board Games

Chinese Checkers, 40-41
Diviyan Keliya, 34-35
Fan Mien, 52-53
Five Eyes, 109
Four Field Kono, 120-21
Fox and Geese, 76-77
Nine Men's Morris, 77-78
Scissors Chess, 107-8
Sugoroku, 115-16
Well Kono, 119-20
Yoot, 121-23

Circle Games

African Blindman's Buff, 15-16
African Game Trap, 18
Baste the Bear, 71-72, 81-82
Battledore and Shuttlecock, 26
Bird's Alive, 71
Blind Hen, 133
Blind Hen, The, 146
Cambio de Instrumentos, 39
Cat and Mouse, 42
Cat and Rat, 30-31
Cattle Stockade, 16-17
Clasping for Seven, 45-46
Color Market, The, 145
Dogs and the Chickens, The, 56-57

157

Dona Ana No Esta Aqui, 58-59
Fans, The, 57-58
Flower Garden, The, 55-56
Follow Through Tag, 99
Fox in the Hole, 75
Fruits, 129
Frying Vegetables, 54
Hanakago, 118
Hanetsuki, 104-5
Kagome-Kagome, 116
Karutatori, 113-14
King's Messenger, The, 37
La Canasta, 38
La Marisola, 65-67
Matandile, 67-70
Nuts, The, 56
Oki Chochin, Chrissi Chochia, 109
Paloma y Gavilan, 28
Priest's Hat, The, 57
Puss in the Circle, 137
Rakansan, 111-12
Rider Ball, 83-84
San Sereni, 60-65
Solemn Action, 131
Va el Tren, 37-38
Wee Bologna Man, 141-42
Wolf, 133-34
Yemari, 106-7

Games Requiring Forfeits

Bird's Alive, 71
Dogs and the Chickens, 56-57
Flower Garden, The, 55-56
Fruits, 129
Hit the Bucket, 75-76
King's Messenger, The, 37
Mulambilwa, 15
Nuts, The, 56
Oki Chochin, Chrissi Chochia, 109
Priest's Hat, The, 57
Turtle's Nest, 125

Guessing Games

Blind Guesser, 125
Fingers Out, 41
Kagome-Kagome, 116
Karutatori, 113-14
Morra, 102-3

Noa, 85-86
Odd or Even, 84
Papago, 25
Poem Card Playing, 114-15
Puhenehene, 86-87
Spreading the Fist, 47
Takara-Sagashi, 107
Where Is the Stick? 22-23

Pantomime

Foreigner, 112-13
My Friend Has Returned from the
    Orient, 58

Racing Games

Ball Race, 22
Jankenpon Relay, 111
Kick the Stick Relay, 26
Lame Chicken, 42-43
Pickup Race, 45

Rhythm Games

African Game Trap, 18
Cat and Rat, 30-31
Chinese Stick Rhythms, 49
How Many Miles to Babylon? 142-43
Va el Tren, 37-38

Singing Games

Dona Ana No Esta Aqui, 58-59
La Marisola, 65-67
Little Ball, The, 128
Little Clown, 127
Matandile, 67-70
Rakansan, 111-12
San Sereni, 60-65
Va el Tren, 37-38

Games of Skill

Arrow Game, 24
Beach Lame Chicken, 49-50
Hit the Bucket, 75-76
Hit the Penny, 31
Kick the Marbles, 53-54
La Palma, 28-29
Lame Chicken, 42-43
Loulou, 87

Otedama, 117-18
Pahee, 85
Potato Joust, 136-37
Shuttlecock, 43
Slap Hand, 110
Spear the Whale, 20-21
Tokinawas, 25-26
Turtle's Nest, 125

Tag Games

African Blindman's Buff, 15
Baste the Bear, 71-72, 81-82
Calah Panjang, 124-25
Catching the Dragon's Tail, 51-52
Coyote and Sheep, 129-30
Cuba and Spain, 60
Gorelki, 139-40
Grinding Stone, 126
"Help!" 132
Hen and Wildcat, 16
Japanese Tag, 104
Kabaddi, No. 1, 88-89
Kabaddi, No. 2, 89-92
Kae Danda, 92
Kho-Kho, 93-95
La Barra, 36
Lame Duck, 137
Lion and Deer Tag, 17
Loo K'bah Zee, 33
Pebble Chase, 83
Puss in the Circle, 137
San Pedro and San Pablo, 135-36
Scorpion's Sting, 92
Sia Mar Danda, 95-96
Smuggle the Geg, 143-44
Takaratori, 117
Tsoo! Tsoo! 41
Water Sprite, 53
Wolf, 133-34
Wolf, The, 146-47

Games for Teams

African Handball, 17
Arrow Game, 24
Buckskin Ball, 24-25
Calah Panjang, 124-25
Cuba and Spain, 60
Da Err, 47-48

Dog Collar, 81
Forcing the City Gates, 41-42
Foreigner, 112-13
Gooli Danda, 96-98
Hana, Hana, Hana, Kuchi, 105-6
Hanetsuki, 104-5
Jankenpon, 110-11
Jankenpon Relay, 111
Kabaddi, No. 1, 88-89
Kabaddi, No. 2, 89-92
Kho-Kho, 93-95
Kick the Stick Relay, 26
La Barra, 36
Lame Chicken, 42-43
Man, Gun, Tiger, 119
Morra, 102-3
Mulambilwa, 15
My Friend Has Returned from the
  Orient, 58
Noa, 85-86
Nsikwi, 16
Papago, 25
Pickup Race, 45
Pima Sticks, 23-24
Poem Card Playing, 114-15
Puhenehene, 86-87
San Pedro and San Pablo, 135-36
Sipa Sipa, 137-38
Smuggle the Geg, 143-44
Spreading the Fist, 47
Takara-Sagashi, 107
Takaratori, 117
Throwing the Square, 44-45
Water Sprite, 53
Where Is the Stick? 22-23

Games for Two

Balito, 100-102
Beach Lame Chicken, 49-50
Catching Seven Pieces, 46-47
Chinese Checkers, 40-41
Chinese Hopscotch, 48-49
Chinese Stick Rhythms, 49
Da Err, 47-48
Diviyan Keliya, 34-35
Dog Collar, 81
Fan Mien, 52-53
Fingers Out, 41

Fist Slinging, 44
Five Eyes, 109
Four Field Kono, 120-21
Fox and Geese, 76-77
Hana, Hana, Hana, Kuchi, 105-6
Hit the Penny, 31
Iau Chhung, 50-51
Jankenpon, 110-11
Jarabadach, 18-19
Kick the Marbles, 53-54
La Palma, 28-29
LaMarelle, 79-80
Lame Chicken, 42-43
Little Ball, The, 128
Loulou, 87
Man, Gun, Tiger, 119
Morra, 102-3

Nine Men's Morris, 77-78
Nsikwi, 16
Odd or Even, 84
Otedama, 117-18
Pahee, 85
Papago, 25
Pickup Race, 45
Pima Sticks, 23-24
Potato Joust, 136-37
Scissors Chess, 107-8
Shuttlecock, 43
Slap Hand, 110
Spear the Whale, 20-21
Sugoroku, 115-16
Throwing the Square, 44-45
Well Kono, 119-20
Yoot, 121-23